A   L

Book
of **Musts**

The 101 Places Every Albertan MUST See

If you think you know
Alberta, think again

Dina O'Meara

TO OUR READERS

Every effort has been made by authors and editors to ensure that the information enclosed in this book is accurate and up-to-date. We revise and update annually, however, many things can change after a book gets published. If you discover any out-of-date or incorrect information in the Alberta Book of Musts, we would appreciate hearing from you via our website, **www.bookofeverything.com**.

Copyright 2009 by MacIntyre Purcell Publishing Inc.

MacIntyre Purcell Publishing Inc.
232 Lincoln St., Suite D
PO Box 1142
Lunenburg, Nova Scotia
B0J 2C0
www.bookofeverything.com
info@bookofeverything.com

Cover photo and inside full-page images courtesy of iStock.
Small pictures were provided mostly by the organizations featured in the book;
City of Calgary: Reader's Rock Garden, Inglewood Bird Sanctuary
David Moll: Rafting the Bow
Ukrainian Cultural Heritage Village: Ukrainian Village
The Village at Pigeon Lake: No Pigeons in this Pie
Edmonton Folk Music Festival: Edmonton Folk Music Festival
Ali Riley: WordFest
Alberta Culture and Community Spirit: Crowsnest Pass
Medicine Hat Tourism: Medicine Hat
Maps courtesy BBCanada.com
Cover design courtesy of Channel Communications.
Printed and bound in Canada by Friesens.

Library and Archives Canada Cataloguing in Publication

O'Meara, Dina
        Alberta Book of Musts / Dina O'Meara.

ISBN 978-0-9810941-2-0

        1. Alberta--Guidebooks. I. Title.

FC3657.O44 2009   917.12304'4   C2009-904602-4

Introduction

During my first winter in Alberta I marvelled at the piercing blue sky on a 40-below-zero morning, then at how quickly my hair, still wet from the shower, froze while I ran to catch the bus. The extremes of this province captivate me, from the remote boreal forests in the north to the treeless Prairies of the south, the rolling hills of central Alberta and glory of the Rocky Mountains to the west. I love that there are scorpions and rattlesnakes in Medicine Hat, a huge swath of sand dunes two hours north of Fort McMurray, and pelicans on the river in the middle of Calgary. But the differences we experience in Alberta aren't just geographical or those of climate.

This province spawned the maverick women who forced an empire to legally recognize their gender as persons, as well being home to arch Conservative Prime Minister Stephen Harper. And where else would you have a museum dedicated to proving the theory of evolution wrong within a 40-minute drive from the biggest exhibition of fossils in the world?

Forget for a moment the Calgary Stampede; Alberta is home to the largest Fringe theatre festival outside of Scotland, and the highest concentration of improvisational theatre groups in the country. Albertans spend more on culture and art than any other province, yet we keep voting in people with apparently limited interest in either.

The thing is we all fit under Alberta's big sky. And the variety of things to do and see is much more than 101 – so please forgive me for not writing about the miracle of Waterton in the spring, the craziness of Sheri-D Wilson and the Spoken Word Festival, or overhearing a conversation in Klingon at Spock Days in Vulcan. Better yet, invite me to visit a favourite place and we'll have a picnic.

This book was made possible in large part by my mother Rafaela Cecilia O'Meara whose adventuresome spirit always inspires and whose loving care keeps me from eating other people's young. Gracias mil, Mamita.

Full-on thanks to publisher John MacIntyre whose vision launched the Book of Musts series, Kelly Inglis for her finalizing touches, and to editor Beverley Ware, under whose skilled hand this reads so well. Finally, thank you to all the people, from live friends to dead famous Albertans, who contributed to making this book a Must Read.

— Dina O'Meara

TABLE OF CONTENTS

ARTS AND FESTIVALS • 7

Cowboy Mystique …Going Big …Edmonton's Fringe …Nuthin' but the Blues …Holger Petersen's Musical Must List …Northern Light Shows …WordFest …Edmonton Folk Music Festival …More Folk Fests …CKUA …Fly with Me …Calgary Folk Music Festival …Bird Watching …

ROCKY MOUNTAINS • 21

Historic Banff …Lake Louise …Chillin' on the Icefields …Fairmont Banff Springs Hotel …Peter Loughheed's Not So Political Must List …Banff Gondola …Coal in Bellevue …Rat's Nest Cave …Jasper …Gwyn Morgan's Outdoorsy Must List …Johnston Canyon …Ghost Lake …Icefields Parkway …Lake Agnes Tea House …Juniper Bistro …Ribbon Creek Hostel …

NORTH • 37

Athabasca Dunes …Cowboy Poets …Alberta Aliens …Oily Getaway …Crystal Plamondon's Must List …dee Hobsbawn-Smith's Must List …Riding the Iron Horse Trail …Lakeland Canoe Circuit …Ukrainian Cultural Village …Grande Prairie …

EDMONTON • 49

A Royal Museum …WEM …Larry Lawrence's Must List …Fort Ed Park …Bernard Bloom's Two-Wheeled Must List …Worlds of Fun …Barb & Ernie's …Botanical Respite …High Level Bridge Streetcar …N'Orleans …Ride the Eddie …Elegance at the Mac …K-Days to Capital Ex …Hawrelak Park …Horses, Horses, Horses …Cycling the City …Blue Chair Story Slam …Turning a Page …Victoria Oval Park ..

CALGARY • 67

Stampede ... Stampede Nights ... The Other One ... Fancy Loo ... Hayato Okamitsu's Must List for the Senses ... Canada Olympic Park ... Catherine Ford's Festival Must List ... Calgary Tower ... Walking Tours ... Heritage Park ... First Thursdays ... Glenbow Museum ... Rafting on the Bow ... Fish Creek ... The Eddies ... Inglewood Bird Sanctuary ... Late Night Eats ... Kalamata ... Calgary's Angels ... Blackfoot Truckstop Diner ... Peter's Drive-In ... Reader's Rock Garden and Café ... Uptown Downtown ... Kilts and Sporrans ...

CENTRAL • 91

Calaway Park ... Gail Hall's Farmers' Market Must List ... Choo Choo Chooboogie ... Tom Tait's Must List ... Alberta Sports Hall of Fame ... No Pigeons in this Pie ... Red Deer ... Rocky Mountain House Light Show ...

SOUTH EAST • 101

T-Rex ... Gopher Hole Museum ... Medicine Hat's a Gas ... Clifford E. Lee Sanctuary ... Diane Wild's Motorcycle Must List ... Windmill Central ... Cypress Hills ... Hog Wild ... Rock On ... Red Rock Coulee ... Horseshoe Canyon ... Lamb ...

SOUTH WEST • 115

Dinosaur Park ... Head-Smashed-In Buffalo Jump ... Fort Whoop-Up ... Full Moon Craziness ... Writing-on-Stone ... Melissa Hollingsworth's Must List ... Mission Church ... Bow Valley Provincial Park ... Jim McLennan's Fly Fisherman Must List ... Crowsnest Pass ... Nikka Yuko ... Twin Butte General Store ... Priddis View and Brew ....

Arts and Festivals

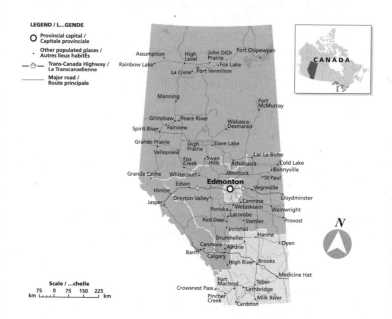

LEGEND / LÉGENDE

○ Provincial capital / Capitale provinciale
· Other populated places / Autres lieux habités
━🍁━ Trans-Canada Highway / La Transcanadienne
───── Major road / Route principale

CANADA

Assumption · High Level · John DiOr Prairie · Fort Chipewyan
Rainbow Lake · · Fox Lake
La Crete · Fort Vermilion
Manning · Fort McMurray
Grimshaw · Peace River · Wabasca-Desmarais
Spirit River · Fairview
Grande Prairie · High Prairie · Slave Lake
Valleyview · Lac La Biche
Fox Creek · Swan Hills · Athabasca · Cold Lake
Grande Cache · Whitecourt · Westlock · St Paul · Bonnyville
Hinton · Edson · Edmonton ○ · Vegreville
Jasper · Drayton Valley · Camrose · Lloydminster
· Ponoka · Wetaskiwin · Wainwright
· Lacombe
Red Deer · · Stettler · Provost
· Innisfail
Drumheller · Hanna
Canmore · Airdrie · Oyen
Banff · Calgary
· High River · Brooks
Medicine Hat
Crowsnest Pass · Fort Macleod · Taber
Pincher Creek · Lethbridge
· Milk River
· Cardston

N

Scale / Échelle
75 0 75 150 225
km km

Tapping into the Cowboy Mystique | 1

The cowboy mystique is alive and well in southern Alberta where ranchers and outfitters continue to ply their trade among the grassy Prairies and rolling foothills, up to the edges of the majestic Rocky Mountains. Why not take a day or a few to become one with your inner cowpoke at one of many working and guest ranches in the area? For city folk who want to indulge in a taste of the rugged life, or for horse and nature lovers looking for an unforgettable vacation, the picks are many and offer a range of activities, lodging and rates. Most ranches are family-run outfits that offer experiences for learners, observers, weekend riders and seasoned equestrians, but some are more focused on either being a working ranch or a guest ranch.

At working ranches learn first-hand why most ranch hands are skinny (it's a lot of work keeping up with the chores), how to saddle up and how to throw a lasso, then fall into a righteously tired sleep in a bunkhouse, or in a luxury (for a cowboy) private room with its own bath. Guest ranches offer similar activities but cater more to the crowd that wants to combine horseback riding with drumming in the woods or a spa treatment, ending up with a gourmet meal or more hearty fare.

Experienced equestrians wanting to explore natural hoof care for their mounts or how to communicate better with their horse can also find courses with certified instructors. For those of you longing for a real trail experience, there are opportunities for real spring or fall cattle drives, including all of the work and unpredictability of running a herd. You'll appreciate the hearty meals and breathtaking views as you ride through the foothills up to secluded mountain meadows even more after a hard day's work. Another option is to go on a pack trip and let the crew do the work while a guide takes you on a ride, hike or to a special fishing hole.

Details: *All those options and more can be found on albertacountryvaca-tion.com and thecowboytrail.com/ranchvacations. Git along, lit'l doggies.*

2   Going Big in Alberta

Alberta likes big; big sky country, big ideas, big malls, big festivals and big-mouthed politicians. Towns in the province also are big on big. We've got giant wagon wheels, baseball bats and balls, ducks, geese, beavers, pigs, vegetables and food, oh do we have giant food.

Take the humungous fibreglass and steel pyrogy at the entrance to the village of Glendon, just southwest of Cold Lake. The fake dumpling, cunningly pierced by a huge fork, is 7.6 metres (25 feet) high and weighs 2,727 kilograms (6,000 pounds). Townsfolk say it would feed 10,000 people if it were real.

Or try on a hungry Tyrannosaurus rex, such as Drumheller has guarding the town. The 25-metre statue is the biggest darn dino in the world, five times larger than the real thing, and hollow inside so you can climb up its absent bowels to survey the town and badlands through its teeth.

Even the remote village of Rainbow Lake, tucked in the northwest corner of the province, boasts a biggie, although you might want to come prepared for the prototypes of Mozzy the Mosquito.

The list of biggies itself is big, so here are just a few of the more noteworthy roadside attractions.

Falher, 161 kilometres northeast of Grande Prairie, commemo-rates its status as the honey capital of Canada with a statue of a bee the size of a compact car. If the insect flew south, it might land on Pinto McBean in Bow Island, near Medicine Hat. Then there's the world's largest Easter egg in Vegreville. The Ukranian aluminum pysanka turns like a weathervane in the wind, even though it's almost 26 feet long and 31 feet tall.

And closing with a personal favourite, the six-ton keilbassa sausage outside of Mundare. The 42-foot statue is a tribute to Stawnichy's Meat Processing, which has been churning out sausages since 1959.

Edmonton's Fringe — 3

The Edmonton Fringe Theatre Festival is a must-see, must-do, and great fun for the 11 days in August where it literally transforms the city to a stage. You can afford to be fussy, but get caught up in the buzz and try seeing as many of the 1,200 shows performed during the Fringe as humanly possible.

Anything can and does go during North America's oldest and largest fringe festival, where more than 200 performers from around the world act out from noon to midnight in Old Strathcona. Half a million people flock to the unruly and uncensored live theatre event that brings acts silly and profound to the intimate venues set up by the Fringe.

There's even a designated kid-friendly Global Family Stage 12 and KidsFringe at the Polynesian Park at the north end of the site for the budding theatrical set. Street performers, crafts and food vendors add to the friendly chaos that characterizes the Fringe as much as the lurid posters hawking different plays.

The festival, the largest in the world after the Mother Fringe in Edinburgh, lets playwrights and actors shake their creative tailfeathers without restrictions. Of course that means some Fringe acts are true duds, and one way to find out which is to eavesdrop on conversations at the beer tent, read the *Edmonton Journal* for reviews, and/or go to festival Ground Zero between 103 and 104 Streets from 83 Avenue to 85 Avenue.

This is the launching point for Fringers and it is here they will find performance listings, a review board, a box office, food, beer and the essential Fringe program. Do not underestimate the importance of this guide to all things Fringe. Not only does it provide descriptions of each play and a schedule; the maps lead you to more beer tents and the loos. Buy One, Keep It Very Close.

Details: *For more information, log on to www.fringetheatreadventures.ca or call (780) 448-9000.*

4   Ain't Nuthin' but the Blues

It's not hard to get the blues in Edmonton, particularly in August when the Labatt Blues Festival kicks in. The three-day blues and mo' blues festival has been sending crowds into indigo nirvana since 1999 with its roster of venerable and new-coming artists like Charlie Musselwhite, Shemekia Copeland, the Fabulous Thunderbirds, Pinetop Perkins and

TAKE 5   HOLGER PETERSEN
A MUSIC LOVER'S MUST LIST

Holger Petersen has been part of the Alberta music scene since he was a fledgling drummer in high school. He founded and runs Stony Plain Records, a label that's won 10 Juno Awards and has been nominated for four Grammys. Holger is a founder and ex-Artistic Director of the Edmonton Folk Music Festival. As a broadcaster, Petersen has hosted Natch'l Blues on CKUA since 1969 and Saturday Night Blues on CBC Radio since 1988. He has received an Honorary Doctorate of Letters from Athabasca University and in 2003 became a Member of the Order of Canada for his contributions to Canadian culture.

1. **Edmonton Folk Music Festival**. We're blessed in Alberta to have many great summer music festivals. This first choice is a toss-up among several, but it holds a special place for me. Nowhere is music, culture and friendship celebrated more than at this laid-back, eclectic event in Edmonton. The daytime session stages are the heart and soul of the festival. And the late-night volunteer parties often include the festival's stars performing relaxed and inspired sets.

2. **CANTOS Music Collection Tour, Calgary**. This non-profit foundation has assembled one of the world's most distinctive keyboard instrument collections. Items range from an early harpsichord (ca 1679), to Sir Elton John and Bernie Taupin's songwriting piano, and the Rolling Stones Mobile Studio — used to record classic albums not only by the Stones but Led Zeppelin, Dire Straits and Bob Marley. If you really want a treat, ask somebody if John is working today - John, who used to be with Iron Butterfly, and you don't need any better creds than that.

Buckwheat Zydeco. And the festival rocks down on the placid setting of Hawrelak Park, just down the hill from the University of Alberta and across the river from some of the ritziest homes in the city.

The brainchild of promoters Carrol Deen and Cam Hayden (also a fixture on CKUA radio), the Edmonton festival stands out for its dedication to all kinds of blues, from swinging Chicago to muddy Delta blues. They also instituted that rarity among open-air festivals; the full-length, 75-minute set. Listening in on the festival is one of the cheapest thrills in town, too, at $75 for a three-day pass, and $35 to

3. **CKUA Radio, Edmonton**. While in the province, check out Canada's first public broadcaster. Started in 1927 (predating CBC) CKUA provides unique 'non-mainstream' programming. It's the glue that holds the province's cultural community together. Heard throughout Alberta on AM and FM, it was the first Canadian broadcaster to go online. Tours are offered during seasonal fundraisers. The music library is spread over four floors and includes more than 90,000 albums, almost 70,000 CD's and 20,000 78's.

4. **The Cowboy Trail**. Listen to Ian Tyson, Wilf Carter, Corb Lund or Tim Hus while driving down the Cowboy Trail along the foothills of the Rockies. Take Highway 22 down to Longview and check out Ian Tyson's Navajo Mug for some coffee and the best beef jerky you've ever had.

5. **Recordland, Calgary.** Worth a stop if you collect vintage vinyl, eclectic music and know what you're looking for. Recordland in Inglewood has the biggest assortment of vinyl in Canada. Mostly overpriced but you can still find the odd bargain. The province has many thriving used record shops run by knowledgeable collectors. I also recommend Freecloud Records in Edmonton.

$45 single tickets, depending on the day.

It's also a great place to pick up CDs and other mementos at the on-site Blues Store, get them signed at the autograph table, then go quaff some suds or snarf a veggie wrap. The festival is a cash-only event, though, so bring green or risk having to wait in line for an ATM that probably runs out of money just as it's your turn.

Details: *Hawrelak Park is located at 9930 Groat Road. There is limited parking on site, but Park 'n Ride buses from Stadium Parkade at the university service the event. Tel: (780) 708-7230; www.bluesinternationalltd.com.*

Northern Light Shows 5

A Kiwi friend of mine thought the world was being invaded by aliens the first time she experienced northern lights. She and her friends were relaxing by Lesser Slave Lake on one of the native New Zealander's first camping trips in Canada when the evening show started.

And that's truly what the aurora borealis is – a gob-smacking, jaw-dropping show of undulating streams of white, red, green and purple flowing in the sky. There are lots of places in the province where the borealis gazing is good, but for easy access and popping colours because of a higher mean temperature, Fort McMurray really has it all.

There are three local outfits which offer excursions outside the city that include explanations of the night sky, constellations and how to best photograph the northern lights. One tour starts in Edmonton so you don't even have to drive the 430 kilometres north.

Before shrugging off a guided tour of northern lights as cheesily tourist, consider the time you tried to take a photo of the lights and failed miserably. The wilderness surrounding Fort Mac provides prime sites for viewing aurora borealis because of the relative lack of light pollution bleeding out beyond the city's borders.

According to experts at the University of Alberta, the epicentre of Canada's oil sands region also lies within the southern portion of the zone of "maximum auroral occurrence" at night. Caused by the interaction of solar wind particles with the planet's magnetic field, aurora borealis is more prominent in higher latitudes near the magnetic poles, and best seen in the fall and winter. Scientists at the U of A also have developed a system to predict the likelihood of a celestial display in the Edmonton area.

Details: *Check out www.aurorawatch.ca for the next best show. For tour information contact Alta-Can Aurora Tours at (780) 452-5187, Aurora Adventures (780) 743-0766 and Aurora Tours (780) 334-2292.*

6 WordFest

Literary buffs and authors alike perk up in the fall knowing they'll able to rub shoulders with some of Canada and the world's best talent at the Banff-Calgary International WordFest. Taking place in Calgary's theatre district and the glorious mountain settings of Banff, this six-day treasure of literary indulgence ranks among the top three festivals in the country. About 12,000 people a year attend the festival and they are treated to literary icons like Mavis Gallant, Greg Hollingshead, Margaret Atwood, Nino Ricci and Roddy Doyle.

WordFest pulls together an eclectic mix of authors, novelists and poets into interactive events ranging from readings of new works, to events for kids in local schools, to hilarious panel discussions on how to survive as an Albertan at Toronto cocktail parties. Being able to hear a favourite author read from her or his latest offering is a major draw of the festival, something made even more enticing because you are likely to have a chance to chat with them.

Never one to shy away from innovation, director Ann Green recently added programming around new trends in storytelling, like blogging and making the leap to film. Having a house band and venues ranging from boozy actor hangouts and art galleries to the renowned Banff Centre of Arts aren't bad selling points, either. While writers need an invitation to take part in WordFest, the public can buy a ticket or pass for a reasonable price.

Details: *For more information, telephone (403) 237-9068 or go online at www.wordfest.com.*

Provincial capital Edmonton and southern powerhouse Calgary have enjoyed a mostly-friendly rivalry since one was chosen over the other to seat the legislature. However, no such rivalry exists for festival talent since both share booking information.

The folks in Edmonton and the Edmonton media knows it's the biggest. And they know too that it was labelled the best folk music festival in North America by *Rolling Stone Magazine*, something it occasionally points out to the folks in the other city to the south.

During the second week of August, the four-day event attracts some 21,000 people a day to its downtown Gallagher Park site to listen to headliners like Steve Earl, Sarah McLachlan, Niko Chase and Broken Social Scene, as well as groove to roots, blues, world, and you guessed it, folk.

The Edmonton Folk Music Festival is a world-class event that promotes all incarnations of folk, from throat singers to punk soulsters, attracting to the festival a huge, multi-generational audience. When not rushing from stage to stage (it's truly a schlep from the beer gardens – I mean, Stage 1 on the east end of the park to Stage 6 on the west end), people just veg out, dance, eat and otherwise socialize at Edmonton's folksiest best.

The festival has the luxury of taking place on an inner city ski hill where no other events take place in the summer, allowing the festival two and a half weeks to set up its eight stages. It also sets up the largest mobile kitchen – the hearth of the festival – in Canada where 2,200 volunteers and all performers and their entourages eat.

Details: *Buy weekend passes early, as in June, since they sell out quickly. And take the bus since the no parking on site rule is strictly enforced. It happens on the second weekend in August in Gallagher Park, 97th Ave and 94 Street. Call (780) 429-1899 or check it out online at www.efmf.ab.ca.*

8   Calgary Folk Music Festival

The fourth weekend of July is a good time to stroll to Prince's Island Park in downtown Calgary and enjoy the cool breeze off the Bow

River, the shady trees, and the highlight of it all ... the sweet sound of folk-roots-funk-world-alternative on offer at the Calgary Folk Music Festival. The four-day event is known as the edgiest folk festival in the province, bringing in the likes of Beija Flor to John Wort Hannam, Ridley Bent to Dick Gaughan, Sarah Harmer and Mavis Staples.

Flush with young folk looking to get closer to up-and-coming independent acts as well as established stars, the festival lays to rest "folk" as kumbayah drones. Of course, the festival's foundation also presents stellar traditional North American, British (big UK fans in the south of the province), blues and world music, in an eclectic, vibrant mix.

Main stage is where headliners strut their stuff, but regulars can tell you it's at the six side stages where the magic happens. That is where you can get a band of itinerant musicians from India jamming with a Hungarian gypsy band, a trance DJ and a couple of Celtic bag-pipe players in a set that has the audience up on its feet. Calgary also offers Folk Boot Camp; three-day sessions by festival musicians fea-turing songwriting, guitar, vocal, and banjo workshops.

Since the island can only take about 12,000 people at a time, Calgary's folk music festival has a more intimate allure (and spurring many an "island" romance) than its older sister up north. Musicians love the shady retreat and the shorter distances between stages and the public love it all.

Details: *Be prepared for every type of weather – one year it hit 30 degrees Celsius then hailed, all in one afternoon. It happens over the fourth weekend in July at Prince's Island Park – access the main gate from the east side of the island behind Eau Claire Market. (403) 233-0904; www.calgaryfolkfest.com.*

Driving back roads in Alberta doesn't mean being stuck listening to bad music or polkas on the radio. Motor along almost anywhere in the province and you can tune into alternative, folk, rock, jazz and classical music, courtesy of CKUA and its network of 17 radio transmitters beaming out its unusual mix on AM and FM dials.

Canada's first educational and public radio started broadcasting in 1927 from the University of Alberta. Since those halcyon days CKUA has maintained its innovative drive, becoming the first radio in Canada to go online in 1996. Listeners are so loyal that when the station was suspended suddenly in 1994, they rallied and created a foundation to help keep the radio and their favourite programming on air.

From Baba's Grooves to Fire on the Mountain, Future Funk to Wide-Cut Country, CKUA's distinctive programming is a welcome gem among radio stations. Indeed, just about everything I know about Alberta and Canadian music comes from listening to CKUA and its dedicated crew of DJs, who make a point of giving air time to emerging as well as established Canadian artists. I first experienced k.d. lang, Corb Lund, Tegan and Sara, the Polyjesters and Wendy McNeill on CKUA.

And the mighty station goes further afield, spinning world music, giving out Celtic cuddles, vocalizing jazz, and belting out Canada's longest running blues program. Farmers and politicians get their say, as do playwrights and poets. The station also produces award-winning history and science spots.

Details: *Tune into CKUA at 580 AM province-wide, StarChoice satellite channel 828 across Canada and on ckua.com around the world on the web.*

10   Come Fly (Fish) with Me

Alberta is a fishers' paradise and features more scenic rivers, creeks, lakes and ponds than you can shake a rod at. There are 600 lakes (300 stocked by our friends Alberta Fish and Wildlife), 245 rivers and 315 spring-fed creeks and ponds in the province to wade into.

Starting up north, you can either drive to a body of water like Lesser Slave Lake, where North America's biggest walleye tournament happens every year, or fly into a more remote lodge or camp, sometimes for a lot less than you might expect.

Margaret Lake, up by High Level in the northwest corner of Alberta, is a favourite among some anglers, where you can find abundant pike, Arctic graylings and walleye. Many northern fly-in camps and lodges fly out of Fort McMurray, where you can contact a swath of outdoor adventure companies for guides, pilots and accommodation.

In the south, fly fishers wax eloquently about the majestic scenery (either mountains or the not-so-distant towers of downtown Calgary or serene Prairies), clear rivers and brown and rainbow trout rising to the bait. Famed guitarist Amos Garrett, who has played with Stevie Wonder, Maria Muldar and Bonnie Raitt, once said he moved to southern Alberta for the peace and the trout.

He's not the only one – a whooping 300,000 recreational anglers ply Alberta waterways in boats, rafts and hip waders each year, contributing more than $350 million to the provincial economy.

Don't let cold weather get in your way, either. Ice fishing (also known as vertical jigging) is a traditional outing for hardy folk with a hankering for a winter feed of fish, and goes hand in hand with other winter activities like snowmobiling and cross-country skiing.

Details: *Before you go, any time of year, log on to the Alberta government website srd.alberta.ca/fishwildlife/fishinghunting/default.aspx for information on licenses and regulations. Or call toll free (877) 944-0313.*

Folk Festivals Not In Calgary or Edmonton   11

With such a short summer season, folk and world music groupies can spend the entire summer going from one stellar festival to another in Alberta. Each one is unique, not only in performer line-up, but in location as well.

The season kicks off with the venerable (1978) old-style North Country Fair, held in the Driftpile Valley, 240 kilometres northwest of Edmonton. This music and camping festival happens the third week of June when days start blurring with nights. Rustic would be the word for the lack of facilities, but intimate, jumping and chartered bus are the real buzz words.

The first weekend of July heralds the Rombs Country and Bluegrass Jamboree in Fairview, about 553 kilometres northwest of Edmonton, a small festival that has slowly gained devotees since launching in 2004. More grey hairs and baseball caps than long hairs and tie-dies attend this lively Peace Country celebration, but the friendly spirit is the same.

Spend the next week resting up, then head south the third weekend of July. The South Country Fair sells itself as a peace-oriented camping, music and arts festival. Located just outside Fort Macleod, about 168 km southwest of Calgary, its mix of local and exotic fare set against the wide Prairies and the edge of the Old Man River attracts about 2,500 people a year.

A week later the Calgary festival kicks off, then grab your banjos and head back north to the Blueberry Bluegrass and Country Music Festival. The central Alberta bluegrass bonanza is held in Stony Plain the last weekend of July and delivers straight up bluegrass, from modern players like Marty Stuart to locals Down to the Wood. Up to 4,000 people enjoy the festival, some camping, some not, which has been called the best organized bluegrass event in North America.

Then it's back south again for the longest-running folk festival in the province, the Canmore Folk Music Festival. Besides being set in the shadow of the Three Sisters mountains, what other festival pipes you on to the grounds? Expect the unexpected, eclectic and boisterous, traditional and avant-garde, blues and world music at this mountain getaway which attracts about 14,000 folks a year.

12   Bird Watching

More than 400 species of birds live and migrate through the province, from pelicans to majestic golden eagles, and there are plenty of places to watch them soar. Because of its unique combination of ecosystems from prairie to boreal forest and mountains, Alberta plays hosts to a wide and diverse range of our feathered friends.

North:
Birders flock to Alberta's northeast and the Peace-Athabasca Delta, one of the largest inland freshwater deltas in the world and the landing site of

hundreds of species of migratory songbirds and waterfowl. Visit the Boreal Centre for Bird Conservation – the only research and educational facility of its kind in the world – and the nearby Lesser Slave Lake Bird Observatory, both of which offer a number of educational and interpretive programs. *See also www. borealbirdcentre.ca, or www.lslbo.org.*

Central:
Beaverhill Lake, about 70 kilometres southeast of Edmonton, near Tofield, is a wetland of international importance under the Ramsar Convention. Hundreds of thousands of geese, ducks and shorebirds visit the large but shallow Beaverhill Lake in the spring and fall, making it one of the favoured stops for wandering birders. See sandhill cranes, red-necked phalaropes, pectoral sandpipers, plovers and American avocets spring and fall. Check out the Beaverhill Bird Observatory.
For more information, go to www.beaverhillsbirds.com.

Mountains:
More than 260 bird species have been recorded in the Banff-Lake Louise corridor where the birding is easy even in winter. In Kananaskis Country, check out the golden eagle migrations in spring and fall at wheelchair accessible Mt. Lorette Ponds.

South:
Check out American white pelicans and American avocets at Lake Newell near Brooks in the summer. Further south, outside of Etzikom, take Highway 885 to Pakowki Lake, to some of the province's best marsh habitats. Swans, cormorants, bitterns and ducks are a common sight at the lake, and you just might get lucky and spot a snowy egret or ferruginous hawk.

The Rocky Mountains

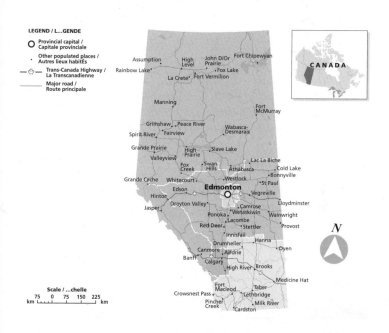

LEGEND / L...GENDE

○ Provincial capital /
Capitale provinciale

• Other populated places /
Autres lieux habitÈs

— ⌘ — Trans-Canada Highway /
La Transcanadienne

——— Major road /
Route principale

Scale / ...chelle

75   0   75   150   225
km |___|___|___|___|___| km

Historic Banff   13

Banff is the quintessential Rockies tourist destination, replete with amazingly kitchy but must-have souvenirs, shop signs in Japanese and over-priced, well, just about everything.

But you can't escape the fact that it is Banff, a town set in the middle of our glorious Rocky Mountains, the ski bum capital of western Canada, a hiker's mecca and where elk still disrupt the traffic on a regular basis.

The town owes its existence to the railways, starting off when the government of Canada promised British Columbia a coast-to-coast railway line to keep it from seceding from Canada and joining the

United States. That train track led to Banff, where three railway workers stumbled on the now-famous hot springs and the rest is history.

To savour some of those past days, take a walk around the Cave & Basin National Historic Site (admission fee required) which is the original hot spot for curative dips. Now you can sniff the sulphur, watch films and play with interactive displays, but no soaking anymore in order to preserve the site.

For a soak, go to the Banff Upper Hot Springs on Sulphur Mountain. Family rates are $22.50 for two adults and two kids for the day when you want to relax after a hike or ski. The spa is delightful.

The Buffalo Nations Luxton Museum on Birch Avenue houses a smallish but unique collection of aboriginal artifacts, outfits and crafts, as well as interesting dioramas.

For some live action, the Siksika Interpretive Centre holds drumming and dancing every Tuesday in July and August at Cascade Gardens behind the park administration building, south on Banff Ave (the main drag). While there, step into the building for some free interactive fun, including simulated shooting rapids on Bow Fall in a birch-bark canoe.

Details: *For more information and maps, log on to the town's official website at www.banff.ca.*

14 Fairmount Banff Springs Hotel

A visit to the majestic Fairmont Banff Springs Hotel takes you back into a time of opulent luxury and the leisurely enjoyment of it. It's a must-stop for anyone in the province – scruffy hiker or moneyed movie star – and a true piece of rather enjoyable history, smack in the middle of Banff National Park.

Dubbed Canada's Castle in the Rockies, this fantastic structure looks down on the Bow River surrounded by forest wilderness and craggy mountain ranges. The sweeping vistas are world famous, and inside is another adventure in turn-of-the-century architecture and whimsy.

The 700-room hotel originally was built out of wood in 1888, and then rebuilt in rundle stone in 1926 after a fire. It has gilded lounges that can fit a two-story house, a host of eateries and bars, cozy nooks to read up on the Rockies in, mysterious passages and cornice rooms reached only by private elevators.

Add a spa, an on-site bakery, a couple of ghosts wandering the hallways and what more could you ask for?

Some of its glory is lovingly worn, but that adds to the old-world charm, along with the floor-to-ceiling windows, little stairs here and there, and sometimes elusive washrooms. The $32 tea might be all you can afford at this grand dame of the Canadian Pacific Railway where rooms start around $290 a night, but it is a full experience.

First of all, there's the setting in the Rundle Lounge overlooking the Bow River and Valley. Then there's the tri-level tray of delectables, including Devonshire cream and scones, of course, along with macaroons, cucumber sandwiches and fresh fruit tarts. Amazing. Reservations recommended.

Details: *About an hour 45 minutes west of Calgary on the TransCanada (Highway 1). Take the Banff/Lake Minnewanka exit just 15 minutes past the Banff National Park entrance, turn left on Banff Ave, then left again off the bridge on to Spray Ave. Call (403) 762-2211; www.fairmont.com/banffsprings. Tip: Go up to Surprise Corner on Tunnel Mountain to get the best shot of the hotel.*

Banff Gondola · 15

If you are afraid of heights, don't test yourself on this eight-minute ride. For one thing, the fully-enclosed gondola is small, seating four adults, and the ride up is quite steep. For another, the round-trip ticket is about $29 per person and for that you can rent a bunch of movies plus get popcorn. But if you're looking to experience views unlike any others outside of a helicopter tour, the gondola and its destination are the bomb.

The wheelchair-accessible gondola climbs almost 700 metres to the Summit Upper Terminal, which is a knee-shaking 2,300 metres above sea level. Once you're at the top, the main observation deck offers a 360-degree view of Banff and the Bow Valley. There are two restaurants at the summit, one on top of the other, with the top one obviously having the best view, and a gift shop.

Hardy folks can stretch their legs and calf muscles climbing up and down the stairs of the one-kilometre Skywalk that leads to Sanson's Peak meteorological station. The namesake, Norman Bethune Sanson, bears mentioning. This dedicated meteorologist made the 3.5-mile hike up the mountain every week for 30 years to record the weather, the last trek in 1945 when he was 84 years old.

Avid hikers can continue up to Sulphur Mountain's real summit following the South East Ridge Trail, and/or pay for a one-way ticket and make their way down the mountain by foot. You also can hike up the mountain, which takes about an hour and a half of concerted hoofing along a lovely scenic trail. The gondola and summit facilities are open year round, and are quite busy during the summer tourist season.

Details: *In Banff, at the end of Mountain Avenue, next to the Upper Hot Springs. For more information call (403) 762-2523 or log on to www.explorerockies.com/banff-gondola.*

Lake Louise is famous the world over for its vista of milky emerald green waters cradled between towering mountain ranges at the foot of Victoria Glacier. The view is spectacular all year round, whether you're hiking, skiing or looking for wild flowers or wildlife.

In the winter, Lake Louise definitely is the place to be for all things snow - it is Canada's largest single ski area, boasting six-person high-speed chairlifts, with more than 100 named runs and some 4,200 ski-able acres. The scenery for snowshoeing and cross-country skiing also is unforgettable.

For a more sedentary winter visit, visit in mid-January for the Ice Magic International Ice Sculpture Competition and Exhibition when chainsaw-wielding competitors create dazzling, complex sculptures from hunks of ice. That the main event takes place in front of the ritzy Fairmont Chateau Lake Louise is a bonus. The Chateau has been revamped and retains a grandeur commiserate to the surroundings. Or curl up with a book in front of a roaring fire at the Lake Louise Visitor Centre where there also are fascinating videos to be watched.

There are two places to shop, at the Chateau or the Samson Mall, where the delectable Laggan's Bakery & Deli is located and you can pick up snacks for the trail. Down the road, the Lake Louise gondola is different from its Banff cousin on so many levels. To begin with, you can take an open or closed gondola and, next, it's a 14-minute trip versus eight up to the much less commercialized top.

For the moderately fit, there are guided walks ($5 a head) and leisurely strolls at the top, with independent hikes to the summit of Mount Whitehorn, or take in indoor films and talks on wolves, bears and unidentified flying objects (usually birds of some sort).

Details: *186 kilometres west of Calgary on the TransCanada, or Highway 1.*

TAKE 5 PETER LOUGHEED
A NOT SO POLITICAL MUST LIST

Former football player and lawyer Peter Lougheed has been credited with bringing Alberta out of obscurity and into an era of political and economic strength during his 14-year tenure as Premier. Under his direction from 1971-1985, Alberta was lifted into the national eye while Lougheed's government created lasting legacies for Albertans. His government increased oil and gas royalties and created the Alberta Heritage Savings Trust Fund (in which a portion of royalties were put in long-term investments) and the Alberta Heritage Foundation for Medical Research. Lougheed's passion to secure provincial control of natural resources did not overwhelm his overall vision for Alberta. A fourth-generation Albertan, Lougheed was equally committed to urban decentralization, culture and education, bolstering health care and recreational opportunities in the province. He and wife Jeanne are outdoors enthusiasts, although at 81 Lougheed admits to have slowed down a touch on the hiking and cross country ski side because of bum knees.

1. **A day in Kananaskis Country**, unequivocally, in any season. What I like most about it is you are so close to nature. What's important is the way we put it together; we didn't build large communities there and you're into the undeveloped areas so quickly and easily. I remember sitting on the side of a hill in the park (his namesake …Peter Lougheed Provincial Park) watching the wild flowers. What an experience.

2. **Hiking and snowshoeing in other parts of the Rockies**. I wouldn't want to specify which areas because there are so many unique places.

3. **Main Street, Alberta**. I was lucky in my former position as Premier of Alberta to do what I called Main Streeting Alberta. Just going up and down the smaller communities, talking to people and getting a feel for friendly, welcoming rural Alberta. It's about the essence of the way they live, the way everybody knows everybody.

4. **The Jubilee Auditoriums, both north and south**. They were built to commemorate the 50th jubilee of Alberta as a province in 1955. My wife Jeanne is very involved in the arts and we go a lot to both; they are marvelous.

5. **The Royal Tyrrell Museum**. It was during our time in government when it was set up, so I have a certain pride of involvement. But more than that, it is unique world-wide. The joy of so many young people, going on organized trips to the museum, is wonderful to see.

Chillin' out on the Columbia Icefields 17

The only thing cooler (ouch) than seeing dozens of glaciers in one day is reaching out and touching one – or better yet, hiking on one, all of which can be done at the Columbia Icefields.

Located almost exactly midway between Jasper and Banff on the Icefields Parkway, the icefield is the largest stretch of frozen solid water in North America south of the Arctic Circle. It covers 325 square chilly kilometres with solid ice up to 365 metres deep. That means it always is cold on the surface no matter how sunny it is in July; so layering up is seriously recommended. The most accessible glacier of the eight major ones along the parkway is the Athabasca Glacier, draping the north face of the 3,491-metre Mount Athabasca. It is retreating at a rate of five metres a year but still weighs in at six kilometres long and a kilometre wide. This one is the glacier you can walk up to a certain point without a guide (beyond lie crevices into which people fall and die on a sadly routine basis) or take a giant six-wheeled Ice Explorer up.

Some folks find the trip a tad understated, but the 1.5-hour tour is fun and informative – and how many people can say they've actually stood on a glacier?

The Glacier Gallery across the highway in the revamped Icefield Centre is one of the best interactive museums in the two parks, featuring a giant glacier model, interactive exhibits and audio-visual programs. The souvenir shop isn't bad either, particularly for collectors of kitchy Canadiana.

Details: *For more information, log on to columbiaicefield.com or call (877) 423-7433. The snowbuses run from mid-April to mid-October every 15-30 minutes. Best times are before 10 am and after 3 pm to avoid the tourist rush. For the more ambulatory, a guided hike can open the world of glaciers in a way the Explorer can't, without the danger, for about four hours, or for the more fit, six hours.*

18   Coal - Bellevue Mine

Alberta holds 70 percent of Canada's coal reserves but just one excursion for people to experience the industry first hand, without any of the danger. Bellevue Underground Mine Tours is the only one in western Canada that takes you a thousand feet into a former mine, suiting up visitors with hard hats and authentic coal miners' lamps to experience the inky depths.

From the moment you walk through the portals of Level 6 toward the darkness ahead – the only lights are the ones strapped around visitors' heads – until the tour ends about an hour later, you are enveloped in the history of the old West Canadian Collieries mine.

Yes, it's an eerie feeling to have the daylight fade behind you and become enveloped in black, smelling whiffs of sulphur from the waters covering levels 7 to 9. The damp cold also increases as the tour makes its way into the mine, dropping to about six degrees Celsius quite quickly, so pay heed when told to bring a jacket. But don't worry about being cramped; the tunnel is fairly wide and high, and flat enough for unencumbered wheelchair access, which is a treat since so many locations across the province are restricted.

Tour guides bring the history of the mine alive with animated stories of the men who worked there and their communities. From 1903 to 1961, miners hauled 13 million tonnes of coal out of Bellevue Mine for its one major client, Canadian Pacific Railway. When the trains were fully converted to diesel, the mine lost its market and closed down.

There also is an excellent virtual tour of the mine upstairs for those who are more comfortable in the sunshine.

Details: *Tours run from early May to Labour Day. For more information, call (403) 564-4700 or log on to www.crowsnestguide.com/bellevuemine. 21814 - 28th Ave, Bellevue, about one hour west of Fort McLeod on Highway 3.*

Rat's Nest Cave   **19**

Most folks think about trekking on a mountain rather than in a mountain, which makes a tour of Rat's Nest Cave, under Grotto Mountain near Canmore, all that much more special than your regular Rocky Mountain hike.

Not only will you be assured of a unique experience, just think about the bragging rights. Okay, so you do have to be fit to go on one of these tours, which starts with a 20-minute jaunt up the mountain. And you're going to get covered in a fine layer of mud, have to squeeze yourself through diagonal folds in the bowels of the earth, and maybe rappel down a 60-foot cavern in pitch darkness to reach the prize. Did I mention bragging rights?

The journey itself, which lasts about four hours through twisting passages littered with the ancient bones of bison long gone from the region, is one jewel in the crown. Guided and geared up by the tour company with hard hat, coveralls, harnesses and headlamps, you will alternately feel, slide and climb down a damp world that stays around 5 degrees Celsius all year round. The inner hike takes you through chambers where dripping minerals have formed icicle-like stalactites and stalagmites to a chamber filled with shimmering mineral formations and a pool of clear glacier water.

Details: *No experience is needed but as mentioned, you do have to be reasonably fit. Kids nine years old and older can come on the adventure, too. Tours happen all year round. For information, call Wild Cave Tours at (403) 678-8819, toll free at (877) 317-1178. Or log on to http://www.canadianrockies.net/wildcavetours. Tip: Don't drink too much before heading out – there are no washrooms on the mountain or in.*

20   Jasper

Jasper is the blue-collar version of Banff, a working railway town that started as a fur-trading outpost in the early 1800s. But it definitely is an attraction, set in the Canadian Rockies' largest national park, a 10,000-square-kilometre wilderness paradise replete with more than 1,000 kilometres in trails.

TAKE 5 GWYN MORGAN
AN OUTDOORSY MUST LIST

Gwyn Morgan was raised on a mixed farm just west of Carstairs, where the Prairies roll into the foothills of Alberta's Rocky Mountains. The wiry, bespectacled Morgan took the lessons he learned at home while making his way up to becoming the head of North America's largest independent natural gas company. Morgan has moved from the challenges of the oil patch to acting as director of banking and engineering firms around the world. The 63-year-old also keeps busy as trustee of the new Dali Lama Centre in British Columbia.

1. One of the things that most distinguishes Alberta is its positive spirit and can-do attitude. It doesn't seem to matter if things are going bad or going well; even at the worse times, people seem to have a resilience and optimism in Alberta.

2. My wife (Pat Trottier) and I are big fans of the outdoors and are backcountry hikers and skiers. The backcountry lodges in the Rockies, just west of Calgary, are so fantastic, both summer and winter. Hiking or skiing in to Skoki (my overall favourite), Shadow Lake or Lake O'Hare is one of those things you should do at least once in your life if you can.

3. Biking on the trails in both Edmonton and Calgary. Both cities have hundreds of kilometres of trails and it's an amazing experience to ride along them. To get out there in a morning or afternoon and just go is a pleasure, you feel like you're right in the wilderness riding along the river paths or through Fish Creek Park.

4. Spend a July afternoon driving through the Prairies up to the foothills, when the crops are coming along and the yellow of the canola, the green of the hay, and the purple of the clover make a patchwork of colour. Driving through this rolling mosaic is one of the great experiences of Alberta.

5. Getting into a canoe and going down some of the great river valleys, like the North and South Saskatchewan rivers, the Athabasca, the Red Deer and the Bow River. Stop and pick some sun-warmed saskatoon berries on the side of a riverbank and experience the amazing changes in the environment between the top of the valley to the bottom. Those river valleys are precious and there's no better place to strum a canoe, especially on a summer day.

Jasper rests in a wide valley where the Athabasca River meets the Miette River, surrounded by Victoria Cross and Maligne ranges, Pyramid Mountain and Indian Ridge. From the town you can hike up trails for half an hour or a week, ski downhill and cross-country, snowboard, paint, fish, ride the rapids and count sightings of cougars, bears, deer, beaver and other wildlife.

Must-sees include a trip to Maligne Canyon, a steep gorge of limestone walls maybe two metres across and 50 deep. There are six bridges that zig-zag down the canyon, the last half for the more athletic. Try the ice walk during the winter.

Maligne Lake, the second largest glacier-fed lake in the world, also is a must, and a 1.5-hour boat cruise along it a bonus. Hold back on that urge to throw yourself in the cold sparkling blue waters though (from experience).

Lake Edith and Lake Annette, six kilometers from Jasper townsite, are two day-use areas with lots of picnic sites and shelters, warmer water for a dip and sandy beaches to dry out on.

Soar almost with the eagles on the Jasper Tramway, Canada's longest and highest aerial ropeway up a mountain. It's standing room only on the tram for vistas of six mountain ranges, lakes and Jasper itself. Be sure to dress warm. From the Upper Station at 2,277 metres, you can roam the boardwalks or take a challenging hour-long hike up to the summit.

Back in town there are lots of quirky little shops and eateries ranging from franchise to fabulous. Take in Fiddle River, upstairs at 620 Connaught Drive, for a Caesar salad with hemp seeds, and the bison and elk meatloaf with juniper berries. Oh, and definitely stop by the Bear's Paw Bakery for artisan bread and scrumptious European-style pastries.

Details: *From Edmonton, take Highway 16 west all the way; from Calgary, take the TransCanada west to Lake Louise, then north on the Icefields Parkway, or Highway 93. Check it out online at www.jaspernationalpark.com.*

Johnston Canyon   21

Johnston Canyon is one of the most visited trails in Banff National Park – and for a number of reasons, not the least of which is its breath-taking location and accessibility. The dramatic power of the water surging through the narrow limestone canyon and the seven waterfalls along the way are awe-inspiring. Being able to feel the spray on your face while on a suspended walkway – which is bolted to the side of the cliff – is another draw.

The half-hour walk to Lower Falls is on easy terrain with a slight 30-metre elevation through lush forest along the noisy Johnston Creek and up to parts where the canyon walls are more than 30 metres high and less than six metres wide. After passing under an overhanging cliff of limestone, you reach the Lower Falls, which plunge 10 metres into a deep pothole below. From there you can either turn back (a pity) or cross the small bridge to the "wet room," a tiny, dark passage carved through the rock by the creek, for a close-up of the falls.

More energetic walkers can go the full 2.7 kilometres (an elevation of 120 metres) to Upper Falls, which is twice the size of the lower falls. The trail is accessible in the winter too, with far fewer people, and a joy to snowshoe once reaching the Upper Falls. The ice formations are spectacular, as are the occasional ice climbers. The canyon trail can be quite slippery, so wear grips on your boots.

Back at the parking lot you can stop into the restaurant for a bite - breakie, lunch or dinner. The menu is selective rather than extensive and, as a result, surprisingly good. The pancakes are yummy, the hot sandwiches fresh, and the dinner entrées quite elegant for the diner-style surroundings. Or stay the night in one of the rustic cabins, which range in price from $145 a night for a basic two-people unit to a $314 per night for a heritage-style cabin which accommodates up to four people.

Details: *From the Norquay Interchange, drive west 5.5 kilometres on the Trans Canada Highway until you reach the Bow Valley Parkway (Highway 1A). Continue on the Bow Valley Parkway for another 18 kilometres to the Johnston Canyon parking lots. Stroller and wheelchair-accessible. Reservations for dinner or a cabin can be made by calling toll free (888) 378-1720 or logging on to johnstoncanyon.com.*

22   Ghost Lake

One of the thrills of winter in the foothills is iceboat racing on Ghost Lake, a beautiful man-made lake lying in the shadow of the Rocky Mountains just outside of Cochrane. Hard water sailing is all about skimming over the ice at high speed in a wee pod that rests on three runners, feeling the ice chips spray on your face as you maneuver the sail.

Created in 1929 when the Ghost Dam power plant was built along part of the Bow River, Ghost Lake is subject to almost constant winds whipping down the valley, making it a mecca for ice sailers from around western Canada. The lake actually is famous around the world because the wind not only fills sails, but it also blows snow off the thick ice, lending excellent sailing conditions from December to about April.

Enthusiasts say the sport is more about the beauty of the scenery than the thrill of flying along at more than 80 kilometres an hour in prone position six inches above the ice. Just watching them race along the lake is exciting for this bystander.

Details: *To get there, take Highway 1A west out of Calgary for about 45 kilometres. Stop by in Cochrane for supplies since Ghost Lake (pop. 78) doesn't have much in the pop or chip department to offer.*

Icefields Parkway   23

Here's a bit of trivia for you: That most venerable of travel magazines, *National Geographic*, rates this Alberta feature one of the "10 Greatest Drives in the World." What drive is it? Yes! The Icefields Parkway, also known as Highway 93, which stretches from Lake Louise to Jasper and back, is a gem of a paved adventure.

The Parkway runs along the spine of the Continental Divide for 232 kilometres of stark mountain ranges, churning waterfalls, more than 100 glimmering glaciers, pristine lakes and lush valleys. Start north from Lake Louise to the Peyto Lake viewing site and the highest point on the Parkway, Bow Summit. There are unforgettable viewpoints on the way of Crowfoot Glacier (a somewhat weird "toe" of ice that clings to the cliffs of Crowfoot Mountain) and Bow Lake at its base.

Move down to the Saskatchewan River Crossing where the mighty North Saskatchewan meets with the Howse and Mistaya rivers. On the way, watch out for the Weeping Wall, a 100-metre-long waterfall which during the winter months is crawling with ice climbers. On brilliantly sunny winter days it's an education in physics watching them skittle around.

Climbing up the Big Hill (you'll recognize it) toward the Columbia Icefields, keep an eye out for mountain goats, elk and maybe even elusive bighorn sheep. Experience the Columbia Icefields, then tackle the last stage of the Parkway, the 104-kilometre stretch to Jasper.

Get ready to see the Tangle Falls, Sunwapta Falls and the roaring Athabasca Falls. These are short, about 23 metres, but the most forceful in the Rockies due to their namesake river that carries the largest volume of water of all the mountain waterways.

Details: *The parkway is easily accessed from Edmonton via Highway 16, Red Deer on Highway 11 or Calgary from the TransCanada or Bow Valley Parkway between Banff and Lake Louise.*

24 Lake Agnes Tea House

When John A. Macdonald's second wife Agnes famously exclaimed, "this is lovely," on seeing a wee lake 7,000 feet up in the Rockies, she might have been fishing for a compliment. Today it's named after her, and home to one of the quirkiest little teashops around.

The Lake Agnes Tea House seats a couple of dozen people inside and a few outside, and is busy all season (which ends on Canadian Thanksgiving) despite having no running water or electricity. All supplies are brought in by horseback (except for the spring helicopter drop) and are correspondingly expensive when ordered on the menu, but oh so tasty after hiking in.

Mind you, the menu is simple, consisting of scones, biscuits, cookies and a couple of sandwiches, all baked in house. The tea selection, however, is extensive and encompasses delicate Asian blends to hearty English teas and local favourites like maple tea.

There is one caveat: You have to hike up about 365 metres to get there. The seven-kilometre round-trip hike is one of the most popular from Lake Louise, and passes forest, grand vistas, and tiny Mirror Lake just before reaching the tea house.

Agnes Lake itself is about a half a kilometre across, surrounded by steep grey rockets of mountain that slope right into its glacial waters. The lake then spills off the mountain lip into the Bridal Veil waterfall.

As for any hike in the Rockies, you'll need to layer clothing as it can be steaming hot one moment and sleeting the next. Which makes a nice hot cuppa just the thing to revitalize before heading back.

Details: *The trailhead is near the Fairmont Chateau Lake Louise. For directions log on to www.banff.com/hiking/lakeagnes.shtml.*

If after soaking in the hot springs, the thought of lunching at yet another noisy pub in Banff makes you cringe, the Juniper Bistro just might be the place to relax and enjoy the view.

And what a view! The restaurant is situated at the base of Mount Norquay overlooking Banff and the Vermilion lakes, with Sulphur and Rundle mountains looming in the background. The terrace is the place to be when the weather is good – if you can get a seat – but inside is pretty enticing, too, with its huge fireplace, hand-crafted wood and stone bar at the lounge, and huge vistas from the south side of the restaurant.

A few minutes from Banff proper, the bistro and lounge are part of the boutique-like Juniper Hotel, and a place where townies go to get a fix of upscale without the downtown traffic. The menu boasts that unique "Canadian Rockies cuisine" which tends to blend contemporary Mediterranean flavours with Canadian favourites such as bison, British Columbia smoked salmon and organic greens and veggies.

Starters and salads are tasty, but the entrees ($25-$34) are what stand out from the menu. The signature dinner is the free-range bison short ribs, a mouth-watering concoction braised in dark ale, with blueberries and organic, yellow-fleshed potatoes grown in Strathmore. But if a nibble is all that's needed, try the goat cheese and butternut squash fritters. Very yummy indeed.

Details: *From Jasper, take the first exit to Banff off Highway 1, from Calgary take the second. Then turn left at the stop sign on the off-ramp on to Mount Norquay road. Follow the road about 64 metres crossing a cattle guard, then turn left immediately onto Juniper Way which will lead you to Juniper Hotel. Call (403) 763-6205 or go online at www.thejuniper.com.*

26 Ribbon Creek Hostel in Kananaskis Country

The Ribbon Creek hostel in Kananaskis Country is a super budget saver, especially for families, whether planning a ski weekend at Nakiska or a spring/fall golden eagle migration tour.

The hostel is set in the heart of hiking, biking, climbing and skiing country, and just minutes away from the ski hill and the ritzy Kananaskis Lodge. For a fraction of the price of a hotel room, you can enjoy the great outdoors, make a rustic dinner at the end of the day, maybe use the gas barbecue, and gather around the fireplace to read or play a game of cribbage.

There's access to more than 60 marked trails, ranking from easy to challenging, and opportunity to explore the foothills and mountains in Peter Lougheed Provincial Park and the Spray Lakes area. One favourite all-year hike close to the hostel is to Troll Falls, an easy walk in the summer to the small glacier-fed falls and a simple cross-country ski venture in the winter.

The hostel, officially called Hi-Kananaskis, has room for 47 people in two dorms plus five family rooms. As with any hostel, the rooms are unlocked and you should supply your own towels. A coin laundry also is a help, particularly after a long day mountain biking.

Details: *The hostel generally is closed mid-April to the end of May and the end of September to mid November. For more information and to make reservations (highly recommended!), call (866) 762-4122 or (403) 670-7580.*

North

LEGEND / L...GENDE

○ Provincial capital /
   Capitale provinciale

   Other populated places /
   Autres lieux habitÈs

─◇─ Trans-Canada Highway /
    La Transcanadienne

   Major road /
   Route principale

CANADA

Scale / ...chelle
75   0   75   150   225
km └┴┴┴┴┘ └──┴──┴──┘ km

N

Athabasca Dunes | 27

If you're up Fort McMurray way, it's well worth the time and effort to fly, canoe or ATV it to one of north eastern Alberta's best kept and somewhat weirdest secret: the Athabasca Dunes Ecological Reserve.

This startling Arabian desert-like area in the middle of the boreal forest is part of Canada's largest active or migrating sand dune complex, covering some 385 square kilometres south of Lake Athabasca. Astronauts circling the globe can see the huge sandbox, but earth-bound folks like us can visit parts of it in more conventional ways.

The trip to the ecological reserve, located about 160 kilometres north of Fort Mac, is worth it which ever way you decide to go. Sliding along the sand ridges, feeling the fine glacier-ground grains between your fingers under a hot summer sky is an almost surreal experience when framed against northern vegetation like jack pines, spruce and tamarack. The sands also meet with shoreline areas along freezing lake waters that include leafy trees like aspen and balsam poplar.

Created some 8,000 years ago, the reserve runs a narrow one and a half kilometres wide and seven kilometres long; the strip contains some of the highest (35 metres) dunes in the world as it transverses the Boreal Shield. Two gargantuan crescent-shaped dunes form the field that feeds thousands of small sinuous dunes that migrate at right angles to the northwest direction of the prevailing winds.

Every year this fragile playground moves about 1.5 metres more southeast, engulfing trees and filling small lakes. It's also one of four protected areas in the Richardson Backcountry region, which includes the Marguerite River Wildland, Richardson River Dunes Wildland, and the Maybelle River Wildland.

There are aerial tours of the region that will take you over the dunes or even helicopter trips that land nearby for a few hours of playtime. Motorized vehicles aren't allowed in the reserve, but there is a short section of trail in the Maybelle River Wildland that all terrain vehicles can enjoy.

Details: *To get there on your own in the summer, follow the Fort Chipewyan winter road to Richardson country trails and campsites and trails leading to the reserve. For more information contact Parks Division at (780) 743-7437, or log on to www.tpr.alberta.ca/parks.*

28	Cowboy Poets

Cowboys are more than just sexy symbols of the open range; there's a sentimental, a humorous and yes, even a lyrical side to those gruff riders. And the best place to experience a spilling of emotional baked beans is at the three-day Stony Plain Cowboy Poetry Gathering each August.

Located 20 minutes west of Edmonton off Highway 16A, the town of Stony Plain lies in prime farmland, home to more dairies than ranches. But since 1992, herds of folks – around 1,200 per each festival – mosey every August to the Pioneer Museum and Exhibition Grounds to experience the joys of cowboy poetry. Really, where else can a fellow describe the throes of love as, "Their eyes take to rollin', their stummicks feel holler, Their goozlums swell up till they can't hardly swaller," (S. Omar Barker) and get away with it?

Part of the gathering's charm lies in its affable atmosphere, where you can bump into an impromptu poetry shoot off while heading to the scheduled artists and downright liars on one of the four stages. It's usually dusty but easy-going, geared towards families, and includes an arts and crafts fair all weekend for die-hard shoppers.

The festival kicks off with a barbecue and dance on Friday night, carrying on to a bonfire gathering where poetry, song and story-telling go on into the wee hours. There's a country market on Saturday morning and cowboy church on Sunday, and poetry, music and tale-telling events both days.

Details: *A weekend pass or day tickets are available online or by phone, but be warned – the festival has a huge following across North America and a history of good weather. Book ahead, both for a place at the RV park or for a hotel room. Call (780) 668-557 or check out www.stonyplaincowboypoetry.com.*

Alberta Aliens 29

St. Paul's motto might be "A People Kind of Place," but aliens are equally welcome as humans are, and even have a place to park right across from the town pool hall. The Republic of St. Paul (Stargate Alpha) boasts the world's first municipally-sanctioned UFO landing pad which hails, "all visitors from earth or otherwise." Even the feds in Ottawa have recognized the unworldly parking spot, located on the corner of Galaxy Way (53 Street) and 50 Avenue.

The landing pad takes centre stage when you drive into town from the west, shod with stones from each province in Canada and topped off by a wall of provincial flags set above a map of our coun-

try. It's a quirky yet tasteful 130-tonne legacy, as is the heartfelt wish for intergalactic peace and harmony noted on plaques in French and English at the site.

The region, lush with lakes and fertile

soil for both farmers and the oil and gas industry, has a long history of UFO sightings. At least that's what some folks, tongue-in-cheek, claimed when tossing around ideas to bring attention to the town during Canada's centennial in 1967. It worked and brought enough tourists to warrant adding a UFO interpretive display, bought from the J. Allen Hynek Center for UFO Studies in San Francisco, to the town's information centre.

The round, glass-encased center is topped off by an archetypical saucer-shaped spaceship as a roof. Inside are spine-chilling tales of unidentified flying objects, photographs of UFOs, and different types of sightings as listed by serious ufologists. There are also photos and explanations of crop circles and other elaborate hoaxes.

Details: *For those of us using more mundane means of transportation, St. Paul is about two and a half hours drive northeast of Edmonton on Highway 28, and just down the road (45 kilometres) from the world's largest pyrogy (see page 8 Going Big in Alberta) in the village of Glendon. Go online at www.town.stpaul.ab.ca.*

30   Oily Getaway

Once a gateway to the west and the fur trading posts along the way, Fort McMurray now is synonymous with big boom and big oil – the Athabasca oil sands, that is. Considered the largest single oil deposit in the world, Alberta's oil sands have gained notoriety around the world for the impact mining and exploiting the vast resource have had on the environment.

Take a look for yourself on a tour of the oldest commercial oil sands operations in the world, the Suncor facilities, or its larger neighbour Syncrude Canada. The equipment used to mine the sticky stuff is as huge as the resource and just mind-boggling to see. Trucks three stories high move payloads of 400 tons every hour around the clock. One operator said it's like driving his house downtown.

Most tours start off at the Oil Sands Discovery Centre where films explaining the history and extraction technologies around bitumen, the heavy oil mixed with sand and clay found in the region. Then climb on a bus to Suncor or Syncrude's operations where you'll see the process from digging the bitumen out of the ground to getting it into a pipeline.

TAKE 5 CRYSTAL PLAMONDON
A SINGER-SONGWRITER'S MUST LIST

The three languages Crystal Plamondon speaks epitomizes her deep, deep Alberta roots. The vivacious singer-songwriter and performer speaks English, French and Cree. Her granddad founded the town of Plamondon in the northeast corner of the province and helped foment her love of culture and music. She is a Cajun fool and is tickled to have been made an honorary citizen of Breaux Bridge, Louisiana. Crystal's other honours include being awarded the 2004 Prix Sylvie Van Brabant for Excellence in Artisque Creation in Alberta. She has been nominated for the Western Canadian Music Award for her album *Plus de Frontières — No Borders*. She has been awarded the Molson ARIA Performer of the Year and has twice performed live on Parliament Hill in 2000 and 1997. 2005 marked Plamondon's lead performance in the musical, "Cow-Boy Poétré," a production of L'UniTthéâtre/The National Arts Centre that toured the Maritimes and Alberta after its run in Ottawa. After a couple years off the road, Plamondon released a new CD, *On a Song and a Prayer,* in 2009 to acclaim and applause as fans welcomed back the Canadian Cajun Queen.

1. Sitting on the shores of Lac La Biche Lake at sunset by a campfire listening to the loons.

2. Sitting by the Highwood River in Kanasaskis Country in the morning watching the wildlife, listening to the birds singing, the fish jumping, having a good cup of campfire coffee and some dark European chocolate.

3. Going to Carlson's on Macleod in High River and enjoying original live music and having a glass of red wine or a beer on the patio.

4. Sitting on the coulees between Forestburg and Donalda watching the eagles and looking down on the amazing scenery where Meeting Creek and Battle River meet.

5. Riding through the forest on horseback or 4-wheeler north of Plamondon in September with the leaves magnificent reds and yellows and the smell of low bush cranberries, while the deer and the moose play.

Details: *Public tours of Suncor's sprawling mining operation are conducted by Fort McMurray Tourism between June and August and are limited to people aged 12 and older. Photo identification is required to enter the site, and certain screening procedures may apply. For folks with deep pockets, there are helicopter tours over the sites to get a true overview of how big the operations are. For the rest of us, regular bookings can be made from Fort McMurray or Edmonton, where you can either fly or bus into the town. For more information, call Fort McMurray Tourism at (780) 791-4336 or toll free at (800) 565-3947; web: www.fortmcmurraytourism.com. Oil Sands Discovery Centre is located at 515 MacKenzie Boulevard in Fort McMurray. Call (780) 743-7167 or go online at www.oilsandsrecovery.com.*

Riding the Iron Horse Trail | 31

The decision by Canadian National Railway to abandon a large stretch of train track in northeastern Alberta has proved a boon to anyone who loves the outdoors. Stretching east from Waskatenau to Cold Lake and Heinsburg, the 300-kilometre stretch is now a multi-use trail used by hikers, bikers, horseback riders, and all terrain vehicle and snowmobile enthusiasts throughout the year.

The line cuts through a landscape that varies from sand hills to pine forests, farmlands to bogs and aspen woods. It passes through or by some 20 communities that vary in size from tiny to city-sized, each with – or without – services such as grocery stores and banks, so plan accordingly. The Iron Horse is a moderately difficult trail that winds through towns and abandoned settlements, over rivers on spectacular trestles and by lakes, offering users an insider view of the glory and history and beauty of northern Alberta.

This corner of the province was the first to be explored and settled by Europeans, and has been used for millennia by aboriginal groups. Besides traversing charming landscapes of rolling farmland and climbing into spectacular boreal forests, travellers will pass by historic sites such as old fur trading posts and landmarks such as the oldest pool hall in Alberta (in Vilna).

Details: *The trail bisects the map from west at Waskatenau to east at Abilene Junction for a 92-kilometre stretch. From Abiline the trail splits northeast for 98 kilometres to Cold Lake and southeast for 88 kilometres to Heinsburg. There are 15 roadside staging areas to start and stop on, giving travellers a wide range of trip lengths to choose from. For more detailed information and maps, log on to www.ironhorsetrail.ca or call (780) 645-2913.*

32 Lakeland Canoe Circuit

Hopping in the canoe for a jaunt around a few hundred kilometres of lakes is such a Canadian thing to do. For those of us who enjoy a placid paddle in the back country without having to schlep gear over boggy marshes uphill all the way, there's Lakeland Provincial Park Interior Lake canoe circuit.

Located in amazingly pristine wilderness about 40 minutes northeast of Lac La Biche, the Lakeland circuit is the only one of its kind in Alberta. It commands great affection and rightly so from the 2,000-odd paddlers a year who'd like to keep its charms secret (not just because of the public carts available at portage points, although for my money it is a huge benefit). The park can hold you on its watery bosom for a few hours or a few days as you paddle, fish and camp through Jackson, Kinnaird, Blackett and McGuffin lakes, with more challenging portages to several other lakes available.

The water is generally smooth, the beaches sandy and the only sounds are those of birds, rustling aspen, spruce trees, and the rhythmic swoosh of paddles in the water. There are seven portages on the circuit averaging 110 metres, except for the 3.5-kilometre trek from the parking lot to Jackson Lake staging area where most folks start off from. That's about an hour haul, made so much nicer with the glorified wheelbarrows.

Novices can hone their skills, but should have paddling basics as the waters become quite choppy when the wind picks up mid-morning to afternoon. Oh, and be aware of bears when stopping off at one of the 29 campsites in the park. The sites are maintained by the province and, more amazingly, have no fees attached.

Details: *There also are no rentals, convenience stores or flush toilets. Bring your own gear (GPS, mosquito repellent, waterproof matches, etc.) and take out your garbage. Follow Highway 28 East out of Edmonton, which then turns into Highway 36 North. Turn right onto 663 East, the secondary gravel highway that leads to Jackson Lake. Telephone: (866) 623-9696; web: www.laclabicheregion.ab.ca.*

TAKE 5 dee Hobsbawn-Smith
A FOODIE'S MUST LIST

dee Hobsbawn-Smith is a chef, writer, author and educator, and longtime advocate for local foods and producers. She is committed to making a difference in how people eat. A Calgarian and fifth-generation prairie resident, dee is the president of Slow Food Calgary and has written three best-selling cookbooks and co-authored two. Her fourth book, *Shop Talk: The Open-All-Hours Insider's Guide to Finding Great Ingredients in Calgary, the Bow Valley and Beyond* (Last Impression), was released in April 2008, and has been nominated for a Cuisine Canada food culture award (winners TBA). In 2006, dee was awarded the MFK Fisher silver medal by Les Dames D'Escoffier. This biennial international award recognizes excellence in culinary writing. dee writes poetry and fiction as well as being a foodie, and is converting her small yard into an edible landscape.

1. **The Peace River ferry at Shaftesbury at dawn.** Any road trip anywhere in Alberta traverses beautiful landscape of one sort or another and in the Peace Country this is especially so. This little ferry ride across the Mighty Peace, just south of its union with the Smoky River, will re-ignite even the most jaded heart. Just as inspiring is a drive into Silver Valley farther west, maybe taking a hike along the Peace's high escarpment in Dunvegan West Wildland Provincial Park.

2. **Bow Lake and Bow Glacier.** Implacable ice, sheer rock faces, green glacial water. This serene spot was made famous by photographer Byron Harmon in the early twentieth century, and it is still a gem, backstopped by the red roof of Num-ti-Jah Lodge and nearby Mount Crowfoot. Pack a lunch and fill yourself — gaze at rock, ice and water, sculpture in its naturally occurring state.

Ukrainian Cultural Village   **33**

Alberta has a long history of luring Ukrainian immigrants to its wooded region, many of whom found the area reminiscent of their homeland at the foothills of the Carpathian Mountains. The Ukrainian Cultural Heritage Village celebrates the hard-working settlers who came to Alberta and laid the foundation for what remains a strong cultural presence in the province.

The award-winning village has 31 old, refurbished farm and town

3. **Eagle Creek Farms, near Innisfail.** There are many gorgeous farms and ranches in Alberta, and Eagle Creek (under the care of young farmer John Mills) is a particularly inspiring one. The fields fall slightly downhill to the creek, and, in the far western sky, the mountains loom. John's sunflower mazes and blooming fields of flowers are gold and garnet faces tilted skyward.

4. **In northwest Calgary, the walking paths in Beaumont Park, on the north side of the Bow River**. In a city not noted for its pedestrian-friendly design, the river pathways are a glowing example of how to make nature a daily urban ritual. This tree-lined stretch in the northwest river valley is gilded by a towering peregrine falcon nest, off-leash areas, a beaver lodge, the occasional coyote and deer, and the sound of water on stone.

5. **Battle River Train Trestle, Fabyan.** Take a picnic and admire history west of Wainwright off Highway 14, three miles west on a road that could masquerade as a deer track. The half-mile trestle towers, nearly two hundred feet above the valley, have been there since its completion in 1909 by the Grand Pacific Railway. On a quiet day, the bawl of a calf echoes through the valley, and hangs on the air for longer than a train whistle.

buildings that one would expect from an open-air museum, typical foods, a gift shop and costumed staff wandering about. But what sets the Ukrainian Cultural Village apart from others is that the interpreters skillfully play real people from real families who made their way across the ocean (largely from 1890 to 1920) to Alberta to settle the region.

Talk about living history: the stories of life in the area at the turn of the past century are based on detailed research from historical records and family lore carried down from generation to generation. So when the costumed person sounds convincing about what he or she did that day in 1912, it's because they're "recalling" something that actually happened. It may be 2009, but you'd be forgiven for thinking it is 1900.

The buildings, which were brought in from neighbouring communities, also came with their own stories, sometimes culled from interviews of people who had lived and worked in them. Farmsteads, rural living and a township are represented on the site, complete with living and working spaces, churches that hold services throughout the season, roadside shrines, shops and schools.

Details: *Open daily from May to the beginning of September, the village runs only on weekends from Labour Day to Canadian Thanksgiving. Events celebrating Ukrainian culture happen throughout the season. The Ukrainian Cultural Heritage Museum is 25 minutes or 50 kilometres east of Edmonton on Highway 16, just 3 kilometres east of Elk Island National Park.   Tel: (780) 662-3640; web: www.culture.alberta.ca/museums/historicsiteslisting/ukrainianvillage.*

34   Grande Prairie

Grande Prairie has the dubious distinction of being the largest city between Edmonton and Fairbanks, Alaska on Highway 43. What the map doesn't say is the county of about 71,000 people sits right on the southern edge of the Peace, that marvellous expanse of prairie and muskeg along the mighty Peace River first explored by European Alexander MacKenzie in 1789.

Close to the city are fabulous opportunities to hike, bike, ride and paddle, or for the more sedentary, just camp out and fish. It's a birdwatcher's paradise, too, particularly during the spring when rare trumpeter swans migrate north to the region, staying until fall. These are honking big swans, the world's largest waterfowl, weighing in at up to 18 kilograms (40 pounds), with a wing span of 3 metres (10 feet).

Each year, Grande Prairie celebrates their return with the Swan Festival at Saskatoon Island Provincial Park. But the best viewing – from afar since the critters are timid – is at the nearby Crystal Lake Waterfowl Refuge.

About 20 kilometers east of town on Highway 34 is Kleskun Hills Park, the eroded remains of an ancient river delta, where a gentle one-kilometre trail leads you through native prairie and badlands, and by a pioneer village. Keep your eyes open for prehistoric mementos; every spring the rains uncover fossilized sea creatures and dinosaur remains.

For more of those, drive 20 kilometres west of Grande Prairie to Pipestone Creek Park off Highway 43, which is second only to Dinosaur Provincial Park in big deposits of dino bones.

In town, visit Muskoseepi Park, a lovely urban greenspace spanning 1,000 acres along Bear Creek Valley. You can camp, golf, go kayaking or lawn bowl at the park, then listen to one of the concerts at the Park Pavilion to wrap up the evening.

Details: *For more information, check out www.gptourism.ca. Head north on Highway 43 from Edmonton, or Highway 40 from Hinton.*

Edmonton

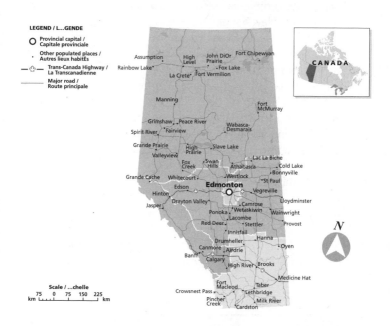

CANADA

Assumption High Level John DiOr Prairie Fort Chipewyan
Rainbow Lake
La Crête Fox Lake
Fort Vermilion

Manning

Fort McMurray

Grimshaw Peace River Wabasca-Desmarais
Spirit River Fairview

Grande Prairie High Prairie Slave Lake
Valleyview Fox Creek Swan Hills Lac La Biche
Grande Cache Whitecourt Athabasca Cold Lake
Edson Westlock Bonnyville
Hinton St Paul
Edmonton Vegreville
Jasper Drayton Valley Lloydminster
Camrose Wetaskiwin Wainwright
Ponoka Lacombe
Red Deer Stettler Provost
Innisfail Hanna
Drumheller Oyen
Canmore Airdrie
Banff Calgary
High River Brooks
Medicine Hat
Fort Macleod Taber
Crowsnest Pass Lethbridge
Pincher Creek Milk River
Cardston

N

Scale / ...chelle
75 0 75 150 225
km   km

Royal Alberta Museum | 35

The next time the kids bug you to go somewhere different and exciting, bug them back and take them to the Royal Alberta Museum where they can handle creepy crawlies themselves. The good folks at the museum have an interactive "Bug Room" with up to 35 live species on exhibit, although only a few, like the giant African millipede (yikes) or the McLeay's Spectre Sticks, are handled by the public with the help of trained volunteers.

Behind glass-encased cages you can gasp at other interesting creatures, such as the tailless whip scorpion, the cuddly Mexican red-kneed tarantula, and more than 300 Madagascar hissing cockroaches, among the largest species of cockroaches in the world. When done with the insects, take a walk on the wild side at the museum's startlingly realistic dioramas of Alberta's wildlife, from grazing grizzlies to hungry eaglets hanging on the side of a cliff.

From there, go to the First People of Canada at the Syncrude Gallery of Aboriginal Culture where thousands of items are displayed in complex dioramas and walk-through displays. The audio recordings, lighting displays and interactive computer programs take you from the last Ice Age to modern day, passing by a bison hunt as it must have been almost 10,000 years ago, and through a tipi to an imaginary meeting of the first European and Aboriginal peoples.

The museum also is a hotspot for cultural events and performances such as photograph exhibits and film screenings, as well as its own special exhibits.

Details: *Buying an annual mammoth pass is worthwhile for Edmontonians and there's a grandparent pass for two grandparents and kids, as well as a family pass. Weekends are half-price and the museum is open daily from 9 am to 5 pm. Located at 12845-102nd Avenue; call (780) 453-9100 or go online at www.royalalbertamuseum.ca.*

36   West Edmonton Mall

Forget the lush river valley, world-famous festivals and colourful Whyte Avenue – a trip to Edmonton without a tour of the mighty West Edmonton Mall is like reading a book during a rock concert, hard to do and just a little pretentious. Because while we all know the mall is nothing but a gargantuan shrine to materialism, its tacky attractions, indoor lake and full-sized replica of the *Santa Maria* are kinda fun. Really.

Enough people to populate two mid-sized cities like Red Deer tromp through the mall each day, depending on the season. It covers the equivalent of 48 city blocks, has more than 800 stores, plus a cop shop, a casino, spas and takes more than an hour to tour on one of those two-wheeled motor Segways.

But what better respite in the depth of a northern Alberta winter

TAKE 5 **LARRY LAWRENCE**
A SOCIAL WORKER'S MUST LIST

Larry Lawrence is a social worker who finds joy and beauty in the luscious Edmonton river valley which runs east-west through the city. Edmonton's river valley is not just one place, but a heavenly assembly of places that look and feel and smell different, that arouse different emotions, that titillate the imagination and the senses differently. As Lawrence puts it, "I never know when I will discover another world in this city." Here are a few, and some of his favourites.

1. The bike trail between Kinnaird Park (111 Ave and 82 St) and the east end of Dawson Park. It is like a Rocky Mountain trail, sans mountains, with bluebells and mossy gardens and birds in the mountain ashes and a rippling brook.

2. In the Forest Heights Park section, through which the east trail south of the Dawson Bridge passes, there are remnants of the coal mines that riddled the valley at the turn of the century. There is a section with a small old spruce forest where the side of the valley is slowly falling away into the river; it creates some interesting effects. I saw a large spruce straddling a crevasse, pulled apart like a wishbone there.

3. In Terwilligar Park I have cycled around ponds and bulrushes to the centre of vast fields of myriad wildflowers and lain down amongst a complex heady bouquet of colours and fragrances.

4. Wild asparagus, picked and eaten immediately, crunchy and warmed by the sun. I'm hesitant to be really specific about where the most prolific asparagus is because part of the fun is the hunt (check out Euell Gibbons' 1962 classic book *Stalking the Wild Asparagus*). Okay, I know I'm being coy. Let me just say that my favourite patches are along the leg of the trail on the north-side of the river between the Capilano Bridge and the 50th Street foot bridge.

5. Mill Creek Ravine. There are several trails that thread their way along the ravine, with numerous pretty wooden foot bridges crossing the creek. There are also the remnants of the original railway that connected the cities of Strathcona and Emonton, including the 1902 Mill Creek Trestle Bridge. The ravine is superbly picturesque at any time of year. Despite the traffic, there are many quiet places to sit near the water. Amazing also are the ice shelves in the spring as the creek thaws.

then to go to the five-acre water park and body surf on the waves? Or tee off at the 18-hole miniature golf course, or check out the African penguins at Sea Life Caverns. Thrill seekers can get their adrenalin levels up all year round at Galaxyland, originally called Fantasyland, the world's largest indoor amusement park featuring 24 rides, including the triple loop Mindbender and other games. (As luck would have it, the Walt Disney Company caught wind of the mall's Fantasyland theme and sued the pants off owners, the Ghermezian brothers, for breach of trademark.)

The mall was allowed to keep the name Fantasyland Hotel for its on-site facility where exhausted shoppers can spend the night in themed suites such as the tiki-tiki Polynesian room with its faux lava rock surrounded Jacuzzi complete with waterfall or the Truck room where for a fee you get to sleep in the bed of a half-ton.

Details: *Located at 1755 8882 170 Street; call (800) 661-8890 or check it out online at www.westedmall.com.*

Fort Edmonton Park   37

Fort Edmonton Park can take a morning or three days to enjoy, depending on your schedule. I suggest more rather than less time. Better yet, come more than once for more time.

The park is divided into four periods of history spanning Edmonton's beginnings as a fur trade post, through to a booming urban centre post-World War I. More than 75 houses, shops, shacks and barracks are on site and you can poke through almost every one. Costumed interpreters are always at hand and fully immersed in the era they're representing; so, go ahead, ask them about what a gal in 1885 would do for fun after the sun has set.

Visitors dive right into history, taking the steam train from the park entrance to the fort from which Edmonton's roots sprang. Perched on an embankment overlooking the North Saskatchewan River, the fort recreates the living, working and social quarters of a typical fur trading post.

Just outside, as it would have been 160 years ago, is the Cree encampment and trading post. From there, stroll down 1885 Street when Edmonton was a town full of dreams but not much cash. At the end of the street, hop on to the streetcar to 1905 Street and an era of growth and optimism before the Great Stock Crash of 1913 and the Big War.

Turn on to 1920 Street for a meal at Johnson's Café, visit the air hanger, Motordome and then take a ride at the midway. Like the midway rides, pony and buggy rides, wagon and stagecoach rides demand a small fee. Feeling peckish? Each era has a food spot, but

TAKE 5 BERNARD BLOOM
A TWO-WHEELED MUST LIST

Bernard Bloom is an Edmonton writer and tutor at Athabasca University. A previous addiction to wandering above the tree line in the Rocky Mountains has morphed into a ferocious fixation on two-wheeled self-propulsion. "Alberta's an active place," he says. "You'll need to move when you're here, but you'll have to choose the right pace. So, pick up a bicycle."

1. Ride the Tour de l'Alberta. It's just such a cool idea. In mid-July, when the Tour de France goes, you can join hundreds of cyclists on a route through the French towns near Edmonton. Alberta's Tour isn't a race; you ride at your own speed on quiet country roads past golden fields of canola, and tour pastures where cows ponder the hordes zipping by.

2. Don't forget the obvious. Take every chance to explore the Saskatchewan River Valley's bike paths. Secluded by cliffs and mature trees, those paths furnish something you don't expect in a boom town.

3. Okay, watch out, here comes the four-letter "S" word! In Edmonton's endless winters, get studded tires and ride silent, pristine streets during a snowfall.

4. During the lovely, warm bits between times full of "S," reward yourself for your efforts with a chocolate-chocolate muffin at the Second Cup on the corner of Whyte Avenue and 104 Street. There you can study youth in micro skirts tottering on stiletto heels and strolling hipsters in stingy brim hats.

5. Finally, don't forget to scold Edmonton's Mayor and City Council about the time they celebrated "Bicycle Month" by removing every bike rack in the city.

1920 Street has the most, from high tea to fast food.

The Fort is operated by the City of Edmonton and as such is a venue for such extracurricular courses as Carpentry 101 for women, heavy horse workshops, party planning and song writing workshops.

Details: *Open daily from the May long weekend to Labour Day. Fort Edmonton Park is located at 7000 - 143 Street, at the corner of Fox Drive and Whitemud Drive. The entrance to the park is located on the north side of Fox Drive. Call (780) 442-5311or visit www.fortedmontonpark.ca for more information.*

38 Worlds of Fun and Science

Whoever said science is boring has never been to Edmonton's Telus World of Science. The World is a veritable playground of wacky facts and interactive exhibits housed in one of the most advanced centres in the world. It's a bright, fun place to be in, full of colourful displays, a planetarium, IMAX theatre and hands-on things to do.

The spacey-looking, wheelchair accessible building on the west end of Edmonton has exhibits that contain secrets of the human body, blast you into space and bring you back to chat with Mother Nature all in one day. Budding engineers can try their hand at programming a robot at the Lego Mindstorms Centre, and amateur sleuths can investigate a crime and process the evidence at a CSI forensics lab at Mystery Avenue. Space Place asks the kinds of questions that are really important, like "What's it like in the Wild Black Yonder?" and "What would aliens think about *us*?"

Or take a trip inside the human body. If you thought Uncle Pedro's nose was big, just wait until you peer up the nostrils of a five-foot honker as you walk into the mouth of the Body House. Inside and all around are comic-book themed exhibits including the ever-popular Gallery of the Gross and body smell jars (double dog dare you to sniff the fart jar).

The littler guys will have fun in Discoveryland playing at the Construction Zone, Waterworks, Potters Corner and other activities. All those mental challenges and intergalactic travel means refuelling; there's a café and eatery on site, as well as a funky gift shop with out of this world items.

Details: *Open daily from 10 am to 5 pm, closed on Christmas and Boxing Day. Located at 11211 - 142 Street, close to Coronation Park. Call (780) 451-3344 or go online at www.edmontonscience.com.*

Barb & Ernie's — 39

Located on the industrial side of the south side of town, Barb & Ernie's diner is unremarkable from the outside except for its old-fashioned sign. But as devotees of this 30-plus-year-old city institution can attest, it's the inside that counts.

In a city that recently named 23-year-old rapper Roland Pemberton as Poet Laureate, pork chop eggs Benedict might seem somewhat incongruous. But not to this crowd. The menu is rib-sticking old world food, with a dash of southern dinner cheek. Add fresh apple strudel every day and Ernie in lederhosen (German leather trousers) on Sundays and what's there not to love?

The restaurant started out in 1975 as a humble joint by the Feuchters that served substantial Teutonic breakfasts and lunch. Barb and Ernie made a name for themselves among the working crowd with their fluffy hotcakes, German bacon pancakes, generous portions and boisterous host. The black forest ham and eggs helped, too, as did the "real white wine Hollandaise" sauce.

Today the kitsch-filled restaurant serves up lunch (try the wiener schnitzel and sauerkraut, with in-house-made spatzle on the side) and dinner, too. Ernie doesn't cook any more but still comes in to harangue the staff (his son Thomas and daughter-in-law Charlene run the joint now) and occasionally the customers. Barb's still in the back though, and has been Ernie's gal since she was 15 and getting ready to be a draftsman and he was 16 and in the middle of training as a cook in Germany.

Hence the munchener schlachtenschussel and the wicked variety of schnitzel for dinner. They also offer a western menu for those not heavy into European specialities.

Details: *Open seven days a week but come early on the weekends or face lining up. Barb & Ernie's is located at 9906 72 Avenue; call (780) 433-3242 or go online at www.barbandernies.com.*

40   Botanical Respite

An annual pass to the pyramids of the Muttart Conservatory is a must for anyone who needs to escape winter's five-month stranglehold on the city but can't afford to move to Kauai. The Muttarts stand out quite distinctly from Edmonton's lush river valley landscape, its two large and two small pyramids grouped like a modern Giza Necropolis.

The pass or a day ticket gives you access to a humid haven of tropical delights where you can replenish from the dry, cold weather outside under a canopy of palms and fig trees providing shade to smaller exotic plants. That is, if you decide to visit the tropical forest pavilion and indulge in the delicate scent of orchids, the flash of hibiscus and bird of paradise, and tropical birdsongs.

The conservatory houses more than 700 species of plants in three distinct ecosystems; arid dessert, tropical and temperate climes, each under its own glass pyramid. A fourth pavilion is for show flowers and changes throughout the year.

Temperature, light and humidity are carefully controlled in all, with plants in the temperate pavilion undergoing a natural cycle of dormancy and active growth each year, only skewered to begin their spring in the middle of Edmonton's winter. Let your mind ponder that fact in the middle of an Alberta cold snap.

Details: *The conservatory offers educational programs for budding botanists, Saturday tours and talks, and behind the scenes at the greenhouse tours the first Sunday of each month. It underwent extensive renovations and expansion in 2009 resulting in more wheel-chair accessible spaces and new educational areas. It's located at 9626-96 A Street; call (780) 496-8755 or check out www.muttartconservatory.ca.*

High Level Bridge Streetcar   41

Drivers crossing Edmonton's High Level Bridge in the summer can easily get distracted by the clickity-clack of an electric streetcar running overhead. But for the passengers riding the vintage Radial Rail streetcar 49 metres above the North Saskatchewan River, the experience is nothing short of exhilarating.

The 40-minute round trip across the bridge allows passengers to enjoy a magnificent view of the city and river valley along what once was one of the highest river crossings by a streetcar in the world. The experience of being on top of everything, cars and water rushing below, is quite a treat, as is waving at bemused pedestrians and drivers on either side of the river, especially after the streetcar exits the only tunnel the Canadian

Pacific Railway ever built in Alberta.

A bigger treat is chartering one of the three streetcars for a private party – after regular runs, of course. Hourly rates are surprisingly reasonable and what a way to celebrate a birthday or get married. The crown jewel of Edmonton's public transit system from 1913 to 1951 when the service was discontinued, the streetcar was started up again in August 1997 by volunteers with the Edmonton Radial Rail Society. They maintain and operate the vintage German, Australian and Japanese streetcars on the High Level Bridge route and at Fort Edmonton Park.

Details: *Catch the streetcar either at its north terminal at Jasper Plaza, 109 St – 100 Ave or the south terminal in Old Strathcona, 102 St. – 84 Ave, just behind the Farmers Market barn. Call (780) 437-7721 or go online at www.edmonton-radial-railway.ab.ca/highlevelbridge.*

42   N'Orleans in Old Strathcona

Dadeo's sweet potato fries should have a notice attached to them when ordered that says, "Warning: Highly addictive." The crunchy side dish at this Cajun diner in Edmonton is almost as popular as its po'boy sandwiches and blackened catfish and, once eaten, is not forgotten.

A standby among the funky and laid back crowd (you have to be because of the waits to get in sometimes), Dadeo Diner and Bar on Whyte Ave. is Edmonton's space-warp to New Orleans, complete with fresh oysters, smoking gumbo and Mississippi Mud beer. Meals here start with buttermilk biscuits and sweet jalapeno jelly and end with key lime pie or bananas Foster. Iced tea and lemonade is served in jars with handles, kitchy décor abounds and mini-jukeboxes belt out an eclectic mix of background buzz.

The eatery is built more for pairs and small groups since, like many of the shops in historic Whyte Avenue, it stretches out in a long, narrow room. Decorated with a 1950s feel, vinyl booths-for-two line most of one wall, a five-person counter welcomes folk at the entrance, and a few four-people booths bring up the back.

Dadeo's is the kind of place friends bump into each other on a weekend, and befitting a neighbourhood diner, the prices are affordable and the staff sincerely friendly. They also do take out, and actually accept reservations.

Details: *Find Dadeo's at 10548A Whyte Ave. Call (780) 433-0930 or check it out online at www.dadeo.ca.*

Ride the Eddie 43

Here's a real deal for the summer-time tourist in Edmonton who is either from away or just touring home turf: The wheel chair-accessible Eddie Bus and its $15 all-day pass – oh, and kids under 12 years old ride free as long as they're accompanied by an adult.

Available late June to early September, the ticket allows you to hop on and hop off at 18 fabulous city attractions then use the ticket for regular transit to get home, to the hotel, or to the car. Although you can board or depart the bus from any one of the stops between 10 am and 6 pm, the sightseeing bus also offers a narrated tour of Edmonton that takes two hours from start to finish.

What's nice about the Eddie is it offers something for even the pickiest traveler, from culture and architecture downtown to shopping funky Old Strathcona and Whyte Avenue. You can stop and stroll around the beautiful gardens at the Alberta Legislature or pop in for a free tour before heading toward the art galleries and eclectic restaurants of 124 Street. After a bite and a coffee, carry on to the Valley Zoo and Fort Edmonton Park.

Details: *Tickets can be bought at major hotels and visitor information centres, TIX on the Square downtown at Winston Churchill Square, located at 9930-102 Ave. Call (800) 463-4667 or go on the web at www.eddiebus.com.*

44 Elegance at the Mac

Dining at the Harvest Room in the venerable Fairmont Hotel Macdonald is one of those experiences that says, "Yes, Jennifer and

Sean [my niece and nephew], you have grown up." The Mac, as locals affectionately call the former Canadian Pacific Railway Hotel, sits like a castle on the edge of a cliff overlooking the North Saskatchewan, giving patrons in the Harvest Room and  on the patio a stupendous view of the river valley.

The quiet elegance of the dining room, replete with high ceilings, warm wood interior and linen tablecloths begs at least a pressed shirt or a stunning pair of shoes. One of the best times to go is just after the noon hour rush, around 1 pm when both front of house and kitchen staff are less stressed. The lunch menu is almost as complex as the dinner menu, showcasing local and regionally sourced items to satisfy both meat eaters and vegetarians. And the prices are fairly reasonable, neither cheap nor outrageously expensive. Lunch items run from $10 to $28, dinner $12 to $48.

Available on both menus, the coast-to-coast seafood chowder has fast become a local favourite with its culinary tour of the deep blue sea. The chowder is topped by Alberta golden trout caviar, and has chunks of wild British Columbia smoked cod, Northwest Pacific shrimp, New Brunswick Atlantic salmon, organic fingerling potatoes and the satisfying salty crunch of wild boar bacon from the Yukon.

Dinner highlights three 100-mile entrees, including "farmer's daughter's" charred grimaud duck breast with duck leg confit and roasted parsnips with spice plum glaze. Or try the organic quinoa ragout, with wild mushrooms, oven-cured tomato, preserved lemon risotto, butternut squash ravioli, and truffle essence. It is regional and organic fare in an elegant local iconic hotel.

Details: *Reservations are strongly recommended. The Fairmont Hotel Macdonald is located at 10065 100th St. Call (780) 429-6424 or check it out online at www.fairmont.com/macdonald/GuestServices/Restaurants.*

K-Days Transformed to Capital Ex　45

Edmonton's Klondike Days used to happen across the city with marching bands and people dressing up for 10 days as either prospectors, saloon girls, card sharks or old time bankers. The kick-off parade still marches on, but the city now calls the celebration of being the gateway to the North the Capital Ex, and it takes place primarily at Edmonton's Northlands. The site hosts a huge midway, chuck wagon races, and attracts more than 800,000 people each year.

They come for the rides (ferris wheel to the Mega Drop), animal shows, fireworks and music – EdFest brings in acts like k-os, Pilot Speed, Paul Brandt and Our Lady Peace, all for the price of the Capital Ex gate ticket. Oh, and for the shopping, like the arts and craft trade show highlighting the works of hundreds of western Canadian artisans. There's also the Aboriginal arts exhibit and the Shop Zone where some 300 people hawk their products and services much the same way they used to during the gold rush.

Just like those faraway times when strange things were done 'neath the midnight sun, vendors from around the globe show off their goods, food and entertainment at an international marketplace.

Families can take the kids to Family Fun Town and mock village, complete with interactive displays like the fire hall where they can check out the gear and shoot water from a fire hose, plus activities and fun rides. City slickers will enjoy becoming country mice for a while at the Fun Town Farm, where guides help kids become temporary farm hands and lead them through the farm-to-market cycle.

Details: *Northlands Park is located at 7300 116 Ave NW. Call (888) 800-7275 or (780) 471-7210, or go online at www.capitalex.ca.*

46 Hawrelak Park

William Hawrelak was the kind of politician journalists loved to cover. The son of Ukrainian immigrants, Hawrelak served as Edmonton's mayor from 1951 to 1959, when he was forced to resign over charges of gross misconduct because of conflict of interest over real estate deals. He rebounded four years later, serving a term and a half before again being booted out of office for shady land transactions. Never deterred, Hawrelak tried federal politics then successfully ran for mayor again in 1974, but died of a heart attack 15 months later amidst allegations of nepotism and influence-peddling.

It makes twisted sense the city renamed a park after the blustery politician, although to this day certain Edmontonians refuse to call the park anything but its former name, Mayfair. Whatever the history, Hawrelak Park is one of the gems of Edmonton's extensive river valley parks system. The 130-acre park slides into a bowl of open grassy areas banked by the North Saskatchewan River to the west and woods all around.

The grounds also incorporate a kidney-shaped lake which is a

mecca for ducks, geese and people with paddleboat mania in the summer time. In the winter it converts to an open-air skating rink, complete with rentals, hot chocolate and choppy ice.

On the south end of the lake, just across from the boathouse, is the Heritage Amphitheatre with its 1,200 theatre-like seats under a great big tent. The structure and the meadow around it is home to events, free and ticketed, such as Heritage Festival, Shakespeare in the Park, the International Blues Festival, and Symphony under the Sky.

Details: *Any time of the year, Hawrelak Park is easy to get to by foot, car, bus and bike. It is located at 9930 Groat Road. Picnic sites can be booked by calling (780) 496-4999.*

Horses, Horses, Horses   47

"But sweetheart, we don't have anywhere to put a horse," doesn't fly as a parental excuse in Edmonton. As most equine-crazy kids in the city know, tucked between the banks of the North Saskatchewan River, Fox Drive and the Whitemud freeway is an incongruous – but delightful – horse farm. To descend into the valley from the bustle of Old Strathcona and watch horses galloping across green fields at the Whitemud Equine Centre is like entering a Zen zone.

The centre has been part of the city's landscape since before it was part of the city (originally as Dr. Frederick Anson Keillor's farm). It's been a riding venue for more than 50 years, the site of Canada's first indoor rodeo and a place where urbanites come to canter along river trails.

Whitemud Equine Learning Centre Association, the non-profit group that runs the facilities, offers recreational riding, riding lessons, courses on horsemanship, camps and tours. People do board their horses in the city there, although the rates are somewhat high. The centre also is home of the Little Bits Therapeutic Riding program, which provides horse riding opportunities for children and adults with mental and physical disabilities.

Details: *Whitemud Equine Centre is located at 12505 Keillor Road, Northwest; call (780) 435-3597 or go online at www.whitemudequine.org.*

48	Cycling the City

Edmonton is blessed with having had people of vision in its history that recognized and made sure to preserve the natural beauty to be found in the city. The result of their forethought is 460 parks — the largest expanse of urban parkland in North America — and more than 150 kilometres of trails, about a third of them bike trails.

The most beloved area to bike in is the river valley where cyclists and pedestrians alike are enveloped by the woodland environment. It's not uncommon to see deer, porcupines, beavers and even coyotes in the valley, as well as other wildlife staggering home from some festival or another.

Rent a bike or borrow one if you are visiting the city, and be sure to hit a lot of the major attractions on your own steam. The paths are clearly marked and connect well from east to west, spanning almost the entire length of the city, from the Strathcona golf course in the east to Fort Edmonton Park in the west, with the legislative grounds and trendy Old Strathcona in between.

Details: *The city takes biking so seriously it provides a slew of information online to bikers, including a free downloadable bike path map and tips on riding in traffic, bike etiquette and bicycling laws. It also gives graphic examples of the different routes cyclists can access and lists bicycle clubs and associations. Visit the website at www.edmonton.ca/transportation/roads_traffic/ transportation_options/cycling-in-edmonton.aspx.*

Blue Chair Story Slam 49

The makings of a memorable dinner party often involve hilarious stories being told shotgun around the table. At Edmonton's Blue Chair Cafe, touted as one of Canada's top 100 restaurants by *enRoute* magazine, patrons enjoy it all during the monthly Story Slam.

Held on the third Wednesday of each month, the often frenetic, sometimes painful and many times weepingly funny event pits the first 10 story tellers to sign up against each other in five-minute slots. Each weaver of fiction shells out $5 for the chance of glory, and the winner, picked by five judges pulled from the audience, takes the pot. The friendly jeers and cheers are taken in stride by the contestants, many of whom are professional scribes who need to develop thicker skins anyway.

During the rest of the month the Mill Creek hot spot lures in clients with its Latin-Asian themed menu (where the curried goat competes with its Pad Thai in popularity) and stellar line-up of roots, jazz and blues bands and singer-songwriters. Owner Harold Wollin books in groups he likes to hear and he has eclectic tastes, from the brazen yet classically minded Stringbean Quartet to the exuberant Pena de Bomba to pensive Maria Dunn.

Blue Chair's tasty cuisine and entertainment is belied by its location in a sad-sack strip mall about six blocks off busy Whyte Ave. Inside, tables and chairs are lined up to face the small (no room for dancing) stage.

Details: *The restaurant, located at 9624 – 76th Ave, is closed Mondays and Tuesdays, but takes reservations (highly recommended) for most other days it's open (festival seating only on Story Slam Wednesdays). Call (780) 989-2861 or go online at www.bluechair.ca.*

50 Turning a Page

For people who love to buy books, independent shops represent an oasis in the middle of big-box retail factories. The deep breath of anticipation that readers take on walking through their doors has as much to do with the knowledgeable staff as with the selection of books and accessories.

Yes, independents carry mainstream as well as alternative books and of course award-winning tomes on a wide range of subjects. But they more often have literature rather than shareholders driving their agenda. Independents offer a venue for unknown and cult authors before they win Pulitzer prizes, as well as reads from local and regional publishers American franchises aren't interested in.

"An independent bookstore like Greenwoods' is a local writer's cheering section at the back of the auditorium, one that holds their lighter flame high during the dark weepy ballads," Edmonton-based novelist Mar'ce Merrell said.

Greenwoods' Bookshoppe in Old Strathcona has been coddling and encouraging bookworms and writers for the past 30 years. The shop has earned accolades for owner Gail Greenwood's direction and selection, as well as for the staff who not only know where things are, but will discuss literary trends and markets. Greenwood's Small World for and about kids is another sweet stop for children and adults alike.

Independents also host events with budding and established authors, run workshops and take the time to gently guide readers and writers toward new horizons.

Downtown, Audrey's Books on 10702 Jasper Avenue has been around since the late 1950s in one incarnation or another, and was originally part of publishing (The Canadian Encyclopedia) and political figure Mel Hurtig's empire. Owned by Steve and Sharon Budnarchuk since 1988, Audrey's boasts two levels and a myriad of events throughout the year, including travel nights and poetry readings.

Details: *Greenwoods' Bookshoppe; 7925 - 104 Street; (780) 439-2005 or toll free at (800) 661-2078; online at www.greenwoods.com. Audrey's Books Ltd.: 10702 Jasper Avenue; (780) 423-3487 or toll free at (800) 661-3649; online at www.audreys.ca.*

Victoria Park Oval   51

Ice skating under a full moon on one of the smoothest outdoor rinks in the city is like moving meditation; the lack of crowds is liberating, establishing a rhythm is soothing, and the benefits are long-lasting.

The oval at Victoria Park, a 155-acre stretch of Shangri-la in the city, is one of Edmonton's best kept secrets. Placed in a bucolic setting with the North Saskatchewan River on one side and trees and meadows to the other, the rink has the bonus of being meticulously maintained because Olympic speed skating hopefuls train here.

The best time to go during the week is after 7 pm Mondays and Wednesdays or after 9 pm Tuesdays and Thursdays (the Edmonton Speed Skating Association has the rink booked in between). The rink lights are on until 10 pm but there's no kitschy music playing and the traffic along Victoria Park Road is hushed, so it's just you and the ice.

The flat terrain also makes the park a great place to snowshoe and cross-country ski. The city provides about 3.5 kilometers of track-set trails through the park.

In the summer Victoria Park reverts to being Edmonton's oldest municipal golf course, with 18 holes and a driving range. It also has a cricket pitch, six picnic sites that can be booked, and a horseshoe pit to play some competitive horseshoes.

Details: *Victoria Park Oval is located at 12130 River Valley Road; call (780) 496-4999. Check www.foundlocally.com/edmonton/Sports/Rec-CrossCountry.htm for other track-set trails.*

Calgary

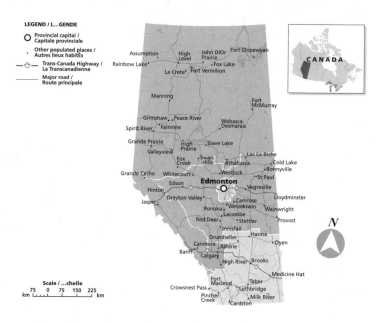

CANADA

Assumption
High Level
John D'Or Prairie
Fort Chipewyan
Rainbow Lake
Fox Lake
La Crete
Fort Vermilion

Manning

Fort McMurray

Grimshaw
Peace River
Wabasca-Desmarais
Spirit River
Fairview

Grande Prairie
High Prairie
Slave Lake
Valleyview
Fox Creek
Swan Hills
Lac La Biche
Cold Lake
Grande Cache
Whitecourt
Athabasca
Bonnyville
Edson
Westlock
St Paul
Hinton
Edmonton
Vegreville
Jasper
Drayton Valley
Camrose
Lloydminster
Ponoka
Wetaskiwin
Wainwright
Lacombe
Red Deer
Stettler
Provost
Innisfall
Drumheller
Hanna
Canmore
Airdrie
Oyen
Banff
Calgary
High River
Brooks
Medicine Hat
Fort Macleod
Taber
Crowsnest Pass
Lethbridge
Pincher Creek
Milk River
Cardston

N

Scale / ...chelle
75 0 75 150 225
km km

---

52   Stampede

"Stampede" is defined as "an act of mass impulse among herd animals or a crowd of people in which the herd (or crowd) collectively begins running with no clear direction or purpose." Humm, say Calgarians, sounds familiar. But there actually is direction and purpose in the Calgary Stampede, a 10-day explosion of mythical and real cowboy culture that takes over the city and its people during July.

Love it or leave it (and many locals do just that), the Stampede is the quintessential Calgary party, created by entertainer and entrepreneur Guy Weadick in 1912 to bring business to the city and money to his pocket. Since then, the event has become the world's largest and richest outdoor rodeo event, attracting top cowboys to a total $1.5 million purse in prize money.

But the Stampede is much more than rodeo; it's about showing off the cowboy duds, and partying from dawn to the wee hours as the city throws itself into western Canada's equivalent of Mardi Gras. It all starts with the Friday Stampede Parade that makes its noisy, fabulously fancy way along a five-kilometre route downtown with more than 170 proud entries of floats, marching bands, trick riders, cultural and ethnic groups, boy scouts and horses.

More than 100,000 people line the parade route, many arriving at dawn to get good seats; so, leaving the core afterwards can be a nightmare. Plan to take about an hour to grab a coffee and wander about downtown after-parade celebrations before trying to leave by train, bus or car – the experience will be a lot less stressful.

If chuckwagon races and rodeos aren't your thing, a huge midway complete with corn dogs and deep-fried twinkies is held on the Stampede grounds, along with agricultural competitions, spectacular shows and fireworks (stake out a place at Scotsman Hill off Blackfoot Trail for a good view).

Stampede also means that weird but welcome custom of free pancake breakfasts throughout the downtown and other community locations, where you might see Prime Minister Stephen Harper flipping griddle cakes in his riding. Usually there's entertainment besides the sight of an executive mixing with the hoi poloi too.

More free entertainment can be had at the Olympic Plaza in front of City Hall, 228 - 8 Ave SE, from 7:30 am to 12:30 pm. Built for medal presentations during the 1988 Winter Olympics, the plaza turns into Rope Square for the Stampede with assorted western activities taking place. For example, the daily mini-parade of First Nations horsemen and women ends its downtown route at the plaza, just before a staged western shoot-out happens.

Details: *Check out local newspapers and stampedebreakfasts.com for dates and places for more information on the Stampede breakfasts. For tickets, event listings, venues and more call (800) 661-1260 or log onto www.calgarystampede.com.*

Stampede Nights   53

Forget about little house on the prairie, Calgary lets it all hang out in July during the 10-day debacle of Stampede, if you trust the spike in April births and divorces filed in August.

Corporations shell out hundreds of thousands of dollars to host their annual Stampede dos, complete with bands like Blue Rodeo and Terri Clark and free-flowing booze. There's a whole industry around setting up Stampede parties (beer tents in parking lots included), but if you can't cadge an invite to a major shindig, there are plenty of parties around town to get down and dirty in.

Ranchman's is the real thing all year round, pretty much the only place in town where working cowboys hang out to drink and dance. They leave the mechanical bull to folks who don't get paid to ride.
9615 Mcleod Trail South.

Coyotes, located by the Stampede grounds, has taken over from its late sister Cowboys as the wild and woolly place to get tequila shots poured down your throat by buxom waitresses wearing cowgirl gear.
1088 Olympic Way SE.

The Whiskey is just south of the downtown core and is the place for cool urban cowfolk who groove to uptown country all night long on its fabulous rooftop patio.
341 10th Ave SW.

Nashville North at the stampede grounds hosts some of North America's best country artists and is a must-do spot for music and dancing – but get there early, as in around 3 pm, or spend time dancing in line.
Ticket office: 1-800-661-1767.

For the laid back country crowd, there's **Buzzards**, where you can hear live music every day, chow down on barbecue for lunch and maybe take part in the Testicle Festival celebrating prairie oysters (bull testicles).
140 10 Ave SW.

And for the too-cool-to-wear-boots crowd, commiserate with each other at the **HiFi Club** where DJs spin breaks and old school hip hop on Thursdays, funk on Fridays and house music on Sundays.
219 10th Ave SW.

54 | The Other Stampede Parade

The Bowness Stampede Parade, held the day after its gargantuan peer kicks off the 10-day rodeo and party event, has to be experienced in person to really comprehend its lack of scope. Sure, you can watch the antics of the Calgary Stampede opening parade on Friday on television if battling 300,000 other folks to get out of downtown afterwards isn't your bag.

But you gotta hang out with the few hundred other locals of this former village who watch, many in their pyjamas, this singular celebration to really get into it. Besides, although it's becoming a bit of a cult must-do, the media hasn't latched on to the Bowness parade yet, so there's no TV coverage.

The parade is led by kids on bikes – any kid on any bike, as long as they're in front of everyone else. Local businesses supported by the local Lions' Club, clubs and residents join for this laid-back celebration of Stampede. This celebration is for the likes of the Ferret Rescue Education Society, local churches, the Alberta PT Cruiser Club, soccer clubs, Boy and Girl Scouts and anyone else who makes an effort.

And if you do, make sure to bring big bags of candy – tossing treats to the kiddles by the side of Bowness Road is a time-honoured and expected tradition. The parade starts at Shouldice Park, heading northbound from Monserrat Drive to Bowness Road, past aging bungalows, a couple of blocks of shops and fading 1970s housing units, wrapping up at the strip mall parking lot on 79 Street NW. And that's where the pancake breakfast, complete with sausages, music, face painting and other fun, free activities take place.

Details: *Pick a roadside spot anywhere between Shouldice Park and 79 Street NW. Bring an umbrella – there's not much shade if it's a hot day, and few places to huddle if it's raining.*

Fancy Loo, a Public Attraction 55

One of the city's recent additions to its roster of "places to take the folks when they're in town," is a toilet. No, really. A $500,000, self-cleaning, automated, stainless steel unit that sends out a piercing alarm if your business takes longer than 10 minutes toilet.

The éclair-shaped public washroom on the west end of Tomkins Square downtown has an electronic sliding door, plays voice messages and elevator music, and boasts a self-flushing throne with a seat that retracts into the rear wall after use.

Then it's like a car wash; the seat gets disinfected while the compartment gets sprayed with water and then fans dry everything off. Motion detectors, which automatically open the door 10 minutes after someone goes in, also make sure there's no one inside before the real fun starts.

In addition to the $469,000 it cost to buy, install and make prairie-winter ready, the municipality shells out another $40,000 a year just

TAKE 5 HAYATO OKAMITSU
A MUST LIST FOR THE SENSES

Hayato Okamitsu is the executive chef of Calgary's award-winning Catch Restaurant & Oyster Bar. The Japanese virutuoso also boasts the prestigious title of Canada's Best Chef after winning gold at the 2009 Culinary Championships in Banff. Hayato has created Japanese-influenced dishes such as Wonton Crusted Tempura Prawns with Togaroshi Dip which quickly became a Catch signature dish and is still the most popular appetizer after seven years on the menu. Hayato is not one to rest on his laurels and he continues to explore a melding of Asian and Canadian flavours resulting in dishes such as soy plum cured Quebec foie gras terrine and the five spice brioche with ginger yuzu pudding. And this hard-working chef is as expressive lauding the wonders of Alberta as he is with its culinary bounty. For Hayato, Alberta is all about using your senses.

1. Visitors and residents alike must **see** the beautiful brilliant blue waters of Peyto Lake, located in Banff National Park. Not only is this lake visually enchanting, but it evokes feeling as well. It was a favourite spot of my mother when she visited Canada before her passing. My wife and I go there once a year to remember her.

2. The must **hear** in Alberta for me is the fabulous live music in the summer on Stephen Avenue in Calgary. It's a real treat to walk down the avenue to work every day with music in the air.

3. If you've been to the Calgary Stampede then you know the must **smell** of Alberta is the many amazing food vendors that feed the crowds every year. From mini donuts, to ribs, to cotton candy, there is something for everyone, and it all smells delicious!

4. It may surprise some that the must **feel** of Alberta for me is actually the powerful and magical feeling of being on horseback. These animals have such a beautiful balance of strength and grace. Although I don't claim to be a cowboy by any means, I enjoy a great guided trail ride while taking in the Alberta scenery, and so should you.

5. And finally, the must **taste** of Alberta is the mouthwatering, sweet, and succulent Taber corn. There's really nothing to say, just eat it! You'll love it too!

to maintain the fancy commode. But business owners, irked by public urination along the 17th Avenue stroll, say the investment of their tax dollars was well worth it.

Details: *Try it for free all day at 17 Ave and 8 St. SW.*

56 | Canada Olympic Park

Sometimes getting out of town for a ski or mountain bike run is too much of a schlep, which is when Canada Olympic Park comes in handy (the lift tickets are cheaper, too). Built for the 1988 Winter Olympics bobsled, luge and ski jumping events, the park stays open all year round now and is an outdoor thrill-seekers' oasis in the city.

Take the 90-metre ski jump. During the winter it's used by athletes perfecting their skills and in the summer it's converted to a zipline, where hardy folks harness themselves into a cable system and zip down at speeds between 120-140 kilometers an hour. Scaredy cats can take the glass elevator or catch a chair ride up to Calgary's highest vantage point and simply take in the view while sitting in the tearoom.

In the summer, COP, as it is affectionately called, becomes a mountain biker's haven, full of kids launching themselves off stunts and jumps, following the more than 25 kilometres of single and open track trails, an obstacle course and trial parks.

Or unleash your young monkeys to the 30-foot climbing wall or the 10-floor Spider Web, a mass of enclosed rubber "webs" kids can crawl up and around in. For adults, strangely enough feeling the need to bounce down the hill butt-over-teakettle while strapped inside a plastic ball, Flip Trip's got it. Not for the faint hearted, the ad says, but great fun to watch. From the outside.

The winter hill is divided into downhill racing, casual and terrain sections, with snowboarders hugging the halfpipe in the terrain part which includes spines, handrails and tables, for those of you who talk snowboard.

For a hefty sum, speed down the Olympic bobsled track in the winter, but you'll have to wait to strap into a luge sled until after 2010 since the Ice House is currently being used by Olympic hopefuls.

Admission to COP is free, activities and programs vary in price. Ordinary refreshments and grub can be had at a lounge and food court at the base of the hill, with a ritzier teahouse at the top of COP.

Details: *88 Canada Olympic Road Southwest or 10 minutes west of the downtown core, at the juncture of Highway #1 West and Bowfort Road. Call (403) 247-5452, or check it out online at www.winsportcanada.ca/cop/index_cop.cfm.*

Calgary Tower 57

Once the tallest building in the city, Calgary Tower now stands in the shadow of a number of gleaming glass and concrete downtown structures. But the iconic statement of unbridled optimism still holds a certain charm, particularly to visiting friends and kids who are thrilled at taking the 45-second elevator ride up and running around the observation deck.

Okay, so it's still a thrill for homies who aren't afraid of heights to stand on the 39-foot glass floor that extends beyond the side of the tower, 190 metres off the ground, with a glass wall in front of them and to see the city and the majesty of the Rocky Mountains splayed out on the western horizon. The sensation while standing on and looking through glass is uncannily like hanging in space, and does bring up the heart rate.

For those of us who favour solid ground, there's still plenty of room for a panoramic view from the rest of the deck, plus opportunities to take photographs, buy souvenirs and mail a postcard from the highest post office in Canada.

For a bit of fancy, there's Sky 360, a revolving restaurant that takes 45 minutes to circle the city. New management did away with a contentious 'elevator fee,' and revamped the decor and the menu to provide contemporary Canadian fare (at slightly elevated prices, too).

The tower itself took 15 months to build and was inaugurated as the Husky Tower in June 1968 for less than it took to build Bill Gate's mansion – a mere $3.5 million. It was the first building in western Canada designed to withstand earthquakes, even though Calgary isn't earthquake prone, and on windy days can – and does – sway up to 16.5 centimetres.

Details: *While the tower itself is open every day except Christmas, the observation deck sometimes is closed for private functions. Located downtown across from the Marriott Hotel at 101 - 9th Ave SW. Call (403) 266-7171or go online at www.calgarytower.com.*

58   Walking Tours

Although much of Calgary is a bit pedestrian-unfriendly, there are several fascinating walking tours in the city that will satisfy the curious and the skeptic.

On Thursday mornings during the summer, you can learn the stories behind the sandstone facades of historic downtown buildings - tales of woe, tragedy and unfettered western optimism told by former Calgary Power engineers and spouses.

The free, two-hour walks are led by members of Projects Organized with Energetic Retirees who uncover tidbits about historic buildings downtown, such as the ornate sandstone buildings along the pedestrian mall of Stephen Avenue.

The guide likely will point out the Venetian palazzo-like architecture of the Doll Block, 116 8th Avenue SE, built by wealthy jeweler Louis Henry Doll in 1907 for his homesick Italian wife. Later that same year, their 10-year-old daughter Florence died suddenly, throwing Doll into a depression that eventually sent him to the Ponoka mental institution.

You'll also hear some juicy stories about Chinatown, Eau Claire, the former site of a lumber operation, and City Hall.

Take a walk on the scary side with Calgary Ghost Tours, a unique company that has researched the city's annals for spooky sightings and stories in five historic neighbourhoods. A caped guide holding a lantern will take you along creepy corners of Kensington, Inglewood, downtown, the Beltline or Union Cemetery and regale you with stories of mayhem, ghosts and local history, like the one about Cappy Smart's monkey Jocko, who was given a full funeral then buried outside Fire Hall No. 3 in Inglewood, now the popular Hose and Hound Pub. Every once in a while the tables start to shake, a phenomena the pub operators blame on "Jocko acting up again."

Details: *For free walks, meet at the front entrance of the Glenbow Museum, 130 9th Ave SE, on Thursdays at 10 am. For Calgary Ghost Tours, call (403) 472-1989 or go online at www.calgaryghosttours.com. Brochures for self-guided walking tours of Stephen Avenue and Inglewood also are available through the City of Calgary.*

Calgary Heritage Park 59

The folks at Heritage Park sure pick quirky ways to bring history to life. The working steam locomotive that chugs around Canada's largest living historical village picking up passengers is one thing. Walking down Main Street and popping into the working bakery for a ginormous cinnamon bun, or the ice cream shop for a lip-smacking sundae is another. And yes, the costumed historical interpreters making jam in log cabins, the rides at the antique midway and the 25-minute tours on a paddleboat through the Glenmore Reservoir also draw thousands of visitors every day during the five-month season.

But the inclusion of an old-time beer brewing course is what won over this prairie girl's heart. Running one evening a month from June to October by Big Rock Brewery's head brewer Alan Yule, the course covers the basics of beer, from recipe to grain milling, mashing, sparging, pitching hops and packaging. Three weeks later, you pick up a bottle of personally brewed suds back at the park. Now if that isn't making history relevant, what is?

Calgary's Heritage Park recreates prairie life from about 1875 to the 1930s and it can take a full day to wander around its 100 restored buildings like the church, sod hut, Wainwright Hotel and blacksmith shop, all of which are staffed by enthusiastic interpreters. The park's newest addition is Heritage Town Square, which features interactive exhibits, shops, the requisite antique portrait studio, the Railway Café and Big Rock Brewery. Another new expansion has been to Gasoline Alley, now a 75,000-square-foot museum that incorporates a drive-in theatre, 67 vintage cars and a 1930s gas station.

Details: *1900 Heritage Drive SW, call (403) 268-8500 or log onto www.heritagepark.ca. A shuttle to the park from the Heritage LRT station runs May to mid-October weekends, and weekdays mid-June to Labour Day. The admission charge for Heritage Park doesn't include rides.*

60   First Thursdays

If you ever find yourself in Calgary on the first Thursday of the month, head to the downtown cultural district for some glorious art, food and entertainment – a lot of it free.

More than 40 art galleries and studios, shops, museums, theatres and pubs within a three-block radius join in and offer discounted or free events during the day, which can last until closing time at a nearby pub.

Each month the eclectic line-up of events changes, from a noon-hour show of guerrilla theatre at the Central Library to a wild (and legal) graffiti painting performance at a local gallery. Things really start heating up at the end of the work day when the studios and galleries at the visual arts hub Art Central bring on the glitz. After five is when the wine tasting, gourmet food demonstrations and metal-work demonstrations or readings start in the refurbished sandstone building.

Wandering through the three levels while live music drifts up the atrium from the bottom floor, mixing with the smell of tasty free tid-bits and the buzz of other patrons, is a creative experience in itself. There's the chance to speak with artists, and maybe get a truly unique gift of sculptures, paintings, ceramics or jewelry.

Around the block and down the road, the Cantos Music Museum offers musician-led tours of its collection of historic keyboard instru-ments for an hour in the evening, a new mystery might be launched at Vertigo Theatre, and a groups exhibition likely is opening at the Grain Exchange.

Details: *To get there, head towards Art Central at the corner of Centre Street and 7th Avenue SW (just remember 7th Ave is the C-Train route, closed to all vehicles except cop cars). You can check out the activities online at www.firstthursdays.ca.*

Glenbow Museum   61

Museums often get a bad rap of being full of dusty dead things and if that's your bag, the Glenbow Museum will disappoint. This is one vibrant clearing house of culture, geared towards being a living conduit into the past that created our present through its colourful and sometimes irreverent exhibitions.

The Tuesday evening behind-the-scenes talks and tours and weekend family-focused events also make the Glenbow a much-favoured go-to place in the city. It's so not a dead zone - Glenbow's collections are brought to life through fanciful and thought-provoking interactive displays which often include sound and movies to add to a full sensory experience.

Of course there are paintings on the walls and strategically placed statues, but they can depict Asian creation themes as much as western ranch life and classical contemporary Canadian works. The museum's five main permanent collections highlight community history, military – kids will love Canada's largest collection of Japanese arms and armour - and mounted police, minerals, Native North America and world cultures.

A big attraction is the permanent exhibit, Mavericks: An Incorrigible History of Alberta. The three-part exhibit borrows the compelling and sometimes tragic tales of adventuresome men and women to walk you through Alberta's history in an interactive format that has you stroll through a railcar or peer into a prairie restaurant.

The museum's First Nations collection also is a big draw, created in cooperation with local tribes. It showcases the art mostly of peoples from the northwestern plains, especially Nisitapii, more commonly known as Blackfoot, Tsuu T'ina, Cree and Anishinabe, but includes Inuit, Northwestern and Metis as well.

Family Fun Sundays are a blast, with activities varying from building a plasticine self-portrait a la Saskatchewan artist Joe Faffard to making quilt squares, and are free with admission or Glenbow membership. The museum shop, like most, is a treasure trove of unusual and fun gift items.

Details: *The Glenbow is open 9 am to 5 pm Monday to Saturday, and noon to five on Sundays. Find it at 130 9 Ave SW; call (403) 268-4100; or go online at www.glenbow.org.*

62   Rafting on the Bow

A raft, a life jacket and thou… There's nothing quite like floating down a lazy river on a raft on a warm day, particularly down the Bow River during Calgary's brief but spectacular summer.

A favourite Bow route starts at Shouldice Park in the northwest end of the city and ends about four hours later just after the Calgary

Zoo in Inglewood (a 20-minute drive by car).

To start, the current of the wide, fairly shallow river lets you drift past the pines and firs of Edgeworth Park with cliffs to the right and Memorial Drive to the left. Most folks skirt around the sand bars and island as the river curls towards downtown, but it's a fun picnic break for others. The current then takes you towards Prince's Island Park, where rafters can enjoy free music during festival season from late June to mid-August.

Once past downtown, the river makes its sinuous way past historic Fort Calgary and the woods by the zoo, where you will want to pull out. Yes, the abundant signs announcing, "Danger! Weir Ahead! Certain Death!" don't exaggerate. Get out on the right hand side of the river following the flow of the river (downstream). There are several well-marked portage points.

Novices might want to check the University of Calgary Outdoor Centre for pointers on rafting before heading out, and go with someone who's been before. The Bow's pretty cold and there are some tricky spots, like bridge piers – avoid them because they'll suck the raft in. And wear the life jacket. No only might it save your life, police actually do patrol the river and hand out hefty fines to people who don't suit up. Wear a hat, too, and carry a paddle. Yes, for the obvious reason.

Details: *No raft, no problem; the University of Calgary Outdoor Centre rents rafts and offers a weekend drop off/pick up service. Sports Rent, (403) 292-0077, and Lazy Day Raft Rentals, (403) 258-0575, do too. Call (403) 220-5038 or go online at www.calagaryoutdoorcentre.ca.*

Fish Creek Provincial Park — 63

There's something both charming and alarming about coming up to a "BEAR WARNING" sign while taking a walk in a city park. The sign goes up every now and again in Fish Creek Provincial Park, where carnivores like bears and cougars have been known to roam. But that doesn't deter folks from walking, skating, biking and hiking through what is one of the largest urban parks in North America.

Fish Creek stretches 19 kilometres from east to west along the Bow River on the city's south end and is about as wide as the city

itself. A hike or ride through the park will take you through spruce forests, wetlands, open prairie and grasslands. Take lots of mosquito repellant in the summer and keep your eyes peeled for migrating birds, deer, beaver and the odd moose.

Paved and unpaved trails will take you to the historic Bow Valley Ranch House (now a fancy restaurant where visiting dignitaries often meet), past tipi rings and bison kill sites, as well as a visitor centre and the very popular man-made Sikome Lake.

More than 20,000 sweaty Calgarians enjoy Sikome's chlorinated waters on hot weekends from mid-June to the Labour Day weekend in September. There are change rooms, food stands and playgrounds, as well as areas for gas-fired barbecues. Pets aren't allowed, though.

Details: *Find Fish Creek Provincial Park at 15979 Bow Bottom Trail SE; call (403) 297-5293; or log onto tpr.alberta.ca/parks/fishcreek/. The Friends of Fish Creek Provincial Park Society run programs throughout the year in and about the park, including talks on wildlife, courses and free interpretive shows; tel: (403) 238-3841; web: www.friendsoffishcreek.org.*

64	The Eddies

Back when Big Rock Breweries was a growing concern rather than the national presence it now is, the clever (and admittedly cheap) executives were casting about for an innovative but inexpensive marketing campaign.

The Okotoks-based brewery, brainchild of Ed McNally, already had tapped into a brilliant way to ship its brews to markets outside of the province by filling empty produce trucks returning to

California. This time they hit on what has become a much-anticipated competition and event for drinkers and non-drinkers alike.

The Eddies Make Your Own Beer Commercial offers fans a chance to show their beer market smarts by creating print and television ads. Irreverence is the key component in the highly competitive and singularly hilarious entries, which stand to win a total of $20,000 in awards.

The competition attracts more than 200 print and video entries, and has expanded to include eastern wannabes, too. Each June, the winning and runner-up commercials are announced and showcased during a raucous celebration of the art of imbibing – an event which typically sells out within minutes of the tickets going on sale.

"The essence of the Eddies is to celebrate our products and spark creativity in our fans," Tara Nychkalo, Communications Manager, says. Attendance at the Eddies celebration has grown to more than 4,000 revelers and includes venues in Toronto and Edmonton. Ticket revenues go to a local theatre group and a women's shelter. Each year the date varies so mark it on your calendar to check. And dress up! It's not mandatory, but attendees are encouraged to match their attire to their favourite Big Rock brew, including Pale Ale and Warthog.

Details: *Big Rock Brewery can be reached toll free at (800) 242-3107 or locally at (403) 720-3239. Take a gander at past Eddies winners on the website at www.bigrockbeer.com, clicking on contests and events.*

Inglewood Bird Sanctuary 65

Folks in the 'hood like to think the Inglewood Bird Sanctuary and Nature Centre is a local secret, but people from all over the city visit the small oasis throughout the year to indulge in its serene wooded trails and chorus of birdsongs.

The 36-hectare pocket of peace has been a designated migratory bird sanctuary since 1929, and is a busy little place in spring and fall when birds and birders migrate through. About 270 bird species have been seen in the area, which is tucked between the Blackfoot and Deerfoot trails but perfectly placed on a bend in the Bow River for feeding and breeding. Bald eagles nest in the area, and a small herd of deer also call the sanctuary home, along with porcupine, coyotes and other woodland creatures.

There are about 2.5 kilometers of pathways in the sanctuary that wind around a small lagoon and by the river, plus strategically-placed benches. More than 340 plant species are found on the grounds, which are open every day of the year from dawn to dusk.

Details: *The Nature Centre heads the sanctuary and is open year round from 10 am to 4 pm or 5 pm, depending on the season. If it's closed, don't worry; there's a gate on the south side of the building (left, from the parking lot) that lets you into the sanctuary. No pets, bikes or inline skates, please. Find it at 2425 9 Ave SE or call (403) 268-2489 for more information.*

Nightclubbers or marathon Scrabble players have limited pickings for late-night noshes in this town where most restaurant kitchens close down at 9:30 pm, but some notable exceptions do exist.

For a full meal until 3 am, head toward downtown and turn right at the imperial lions. Calgary's Chinatown is the third largest in Canada, after Vancouver and Toronto, and a late night favourite for gamblers and hungry lovers is the **Golden Inn**. Rather Spartan in décor, the Inn serves some of the best salt and pepper squid in the city, at any hour of the day, and has a solid Cantonese menu.
107 2nd Ave SE.

For plain grub until around 4 am (on weekends) hip nighthawks circle around **Tubby Dog** on trendy 17th Ave SW. Devotees swear by its oddball fixings, like Capt'n Crunch, wasabi and toasted sesame seeds, and its pinball table. More plebeian Ukrainian sausage and even decent veggie dogs also are available, with sides of onion rings, yam and potato fries.
1022 17 Ave SW.

Across the river, Japanese eatery **Shibuya Izakaya** keeps its kitchen open until 2 am, serving up some of the best ramen (noodles in broth) in town. They specialize in smaller meal options, kind of like Japanese tapas, making this a fab place to sip sake and fill up on exotic finger food.
449 16 Ave NE.

Shawarma Palace, up by Forest Lawn, stays open until 4 am, and like the sign says, serves up a mean Lebanese-style chicken or beef pita wrap. Customers drift in and out all night, and it's a favourite break spot for weary cab drivers.
3820 17 Ave SE.

Kalamata   67

Just on the edge of the downtown core, Kalamata Grocery is an oasis of other-world funkiness. The Greek grocery's plain façade belies the bargain-priced delights to be found within. Even the regular convenience store fare of canned soup and dusty dried goods is from away, as in Turkey, Greece, Bulgaria, Egypt and Lebanon.

    The corner store has been owned and run by the Kokos family

TAKE 5 CATHERINE FORD
A FESTIVAL MUST LIST

Catherine Ford is an outspoken, brash, suffer-no-fools-gladly person who also is an unabashed fan of Alberta where her roots span three generations. Her non-fiction book, *Against the Grain: An Irreverent View of Alberta*, was published in 2004 and quickly became a bestseller. A journalist for 40 years, national columnist and former Associate Editor of the *Calgary Herald*, Ford has worked across Canada but always returned to Calgary. She has earned a multitude of awards including the National Media Award for the Canadian Association for the Advancement for Women and Sport, and the 2006 Freedom of Expression award. One of Catherine's favourite things to do in Alberta is smashing the myth that all culture in the province has to do with farming or ranching. Here are five of the many weapons she uses to do so.

1. **Windy Mountain Music, the Fort Macleod Chamber Music Festival**. It's the most unlikely venue for what is, in fact, world-class music. It just blows me away – every year my husband and I make the trek, stay for the weekend, usually the last weekend in May, and enjoy the classical music by international and local musicians. It's brilliant.

2. **Decidedly Jazz Danceworks**. They bring a New York perspective to Calgary in that they do stuff that is edgy and not necessarily crowd-pleasing, although I always like their work. The experimental nature of DJD can only be achieved by being very confident of who and what the troupe is.

3. **Alberta Theatre Projects**. They try to bring new plays into Alberta. We are inundated with old Broadway plays and musicals and I want to support local artists and Canadian plays.

4. **The Calgary Stampede**. You can't talk culture in Alberta without the Stampede. But the underside of the Calgary Stampede is the agricultural part. I love being able to go, in the middle of a city of a million people, and wander through things you might never have seen, like a cow face-to-face – that's all part of the exhibition. And if you think that the Stampede is all white, male or blonde, all you have to do is go to the grounds and stand in one spot. The world will pass you by. This is truly the face of Calgary and it is people from all over the world, all different colours, all enjoying the same thing.

5. When I want to escape, there are **the mountains**. My roots and my husband's roots in Alberta are really deep. I lived for a while in eastern Canada and it was great, but the one thing I missed and had to come back for was the mountains. I'm not a hiker or a skier, but there's something so peaceful about being in the mountains. Crowds of people hem me in – mountains envelope me; I feel cosseted by them.

since 1965, and on Sundays you'll find the third generation running the till. The isles are narrow and dark, and the shelves packed with surprises like spongy injera, the Eritrean bread made out of teff flour, and Argentine Yerba Mate, as well as olive oil hand soap and Turkish Delight.

"I love coming here, even if I don't know what half of this stuff is," downtowner Sinead Casey says. One of the biggest draws for regulars is the barrel of feta which customers from across the city swear holds the freshest Greek feta in town. It's right at the entrance, just behind the deli counter full of delectable olives (10 types plain, eight types stuffed – the green olive stuffed with almonds is a local favourite), stuffed grape leaves and fried eggplant. Add a wide assortment of olives, bulk and canned, and mouth-watering baklava to mix and opa! You've got the makings and the mood for a tasty Mediterranean mezza.

Details: *The hours are convenient too; 8 am to 11 pm, seven days a week. Find Kalamata at 1421 11 Street SW or call (403) 244-0220.*

68 Calgary's Angels

Angel's Drive-in is more than a funky little diner perched on a corner of what used to be the village of Bowness; it's a neighbourhood institution. Angel's is the kind of place where you ring a door bell at the drive-in window to get service and get greeted by your name.

Kids throw their bikes down by the picnic tables before lining up with earnest faces to order ice cream, and every Wednesday is classic car and hot rod night. The tiny trailer-shaped building has a definite retro-theme going, from its vinyl booths and table-top jukeboxes to the framed pictures of hot rods that line the wall.

The menu is pure diner; hamburgers, deep fried things, classic breakfasts, sandwiches and lunches, and Angel's delightful shakes, soft cones and banana splits. Prices are retro, too, with the most expensive items, apart from the family-sized picnic buckets of fried chicken, costing $8.50, hot entrees served with fries.

Angel's has been owned and operated by Zaher Najar since 2000, when he and his brothers Omar and Shadi decided to move from running another burger place in Raymond, Saskatchewan to Calgary. Najar loves operating an old-style business where he knows his customers and they feel comfortable enough to pile in for a fresh fruit shake after getting hitched in the nearby park.

Details: *Try to make it for the first Saturday in July when Najar hosts Music on the Roof, where two local bands get hauled up the asphalt roof and play from around noon to "whenever they're done." Find Angel's at 8603 - 47 Avenue NW; call (403) 288-1009 or log on to www.angelsdrivein.com.*

Blackfoot Truckstop Diner | 69

Calgarians are notoriously fickle when it comes to patronizing eateries for more than three months at a time. But one tried-and-true landmark in the city has been feeding hungry hoards for the past 50 years, and 24 hours a day at that.

The Blackfoot Truckstop Diner at the east end of trendy Inglewood has been catering to long-distance haulers, hung-over students and insomniacs alike since 1956. The Highway 66 atmosphere is pure blue-collar family and owner Edna Taylor and her cadre of pink-uniformed, 80s-permed waitresses keep it that way.

"Want something to drink, sweetie?" is the welcome call by staff, most of whom have been working at the diner for at least a decade or two.

Edna, a petite 79-year-old dynamo, bustles about making sure everything's running smoothly, and chatting with the patrons who vary from lap top-toting executives to city workers, truckers, retirees and cab drivers. She feeds the odd penniless visitor, but says the truckers do more. "They're all just ordinary people," she says, "people who help other people."

Patrons dig into the diner's home-style food like the CPR Special Breakfast of sausage or ham, perogies, eggs and toast, the clubhouse sandwiches and the pies. Yes, the pies. Like the Flapper Pie, with its mile-high meringue on a graham cracker crust, or the lemon meringue, all made in-house.

Details: *Visit the Blackfoot Truckstop Diner at 1840 9 Ave. SE or call (403) 265-5964.*

There are no chicken burgers to be had at Peters' Drive-In, nor any fancy salads. In fact, there are no salads at all on the menu at this landmark burger-and-fries joint off the busy 16th Ave NW. The lack of veggies doesn't deter hundreds of people from lining up for Peters' barbecue sauce covered burgers and yummy shakes. They definitely don't come for the location, which is right off the TransCanada Highway where thousands of vehicles pass through town.

But the site is picturesque in a worn-out nostalgic kind of way, with its picnic tables, packed parking lot and flocks of savvy gulls waiting for leftovers. Most of the staff has worked there for years, a living legacy of late founder Gus Pieters' philosophy of keeping things simple and paying people their worth.

The menu hasn't changed much in forty years because "why mess with success," Pieters once said. There are single (actually a single and a half), double and triple burgers, plain or with cheese. Regular cheddar cheese, mind you, none of this fancy blue or goat cheese for this burger palace. Hot dogs and cheese dogs and small and large fries compliment the menu, as do the absolutely best onion rings in town. These babies are thin, crispy and crunchy with just the right amount of oil to fulfill the need.

The coupe de grace for many is Peters' milkshakes. Made with real fruit, there's no extra charge to mix, say, a coconut, mango and root beer shake, from a one-flavour shake. There's just one size: huge. The sundae menu is classic as well, with a choice of butterscotch, chocolate, hot fudge, marshmallow and pineapple.

Details: *The old fashioned atmosphere extends to Peters' accepting only cash, no Visa or debt card. No reservations taken. Located at 219 16 Ave NW; tel: (403) 277-2747; web: www.petersdrivein.com.*

Reader's Rock Garden and Café

Just across the street from the perennially busy Stampede grounds entrance on 25th Ave and Mcleod Trail, there's a little sign that says "Reader's Rock Garden." Most people miss it because the sign is right by the north end of Union Cemetery and how interesting could a rock garden by a bone yard be? Not only interesting and beautiful, the garden guards one of the town's best-kept secrets – Reader's Garden Café.

Ensconced at the top of the hill, the café is completely shrouded from the rest of the city by a veil of trees and greenery, although patrons sitting on the veranda can see the Stampede grounds to the north.

The 40-odd seat restaurant occupies the main floor of a perfect replica of the original pre-First World War arts and crafts home built on site, constructed following the original blueprints. The menu showcases regional garden fare such as soups with organic greens, trout and bison smoked in nearby Millarville, and salads with edible flowers grown in the café garden. There are a couple of ways to get to the café, the best being the winding trail through the garden up the hill from the parking lot.

William Roland Reader, Calgary Parks superintendent from 1913 to 1942, created the garden over three decades, transforming a barren prairie hillside to an internationally acclaimed garden. Reader and his friends would bring plants back from travels in the region and the world, eventually trialing more than 4,000 species. The garden grew in disarray after Reader's death and its trees and flowers pillaged. The site was rehabilitated in early 2000 and the café opened soon after.

Details: *The restaurant is open daily from mid-May to mid-October 11 am to 9 pm and is wheelchair accessible via Spiller Road on the east side of the cemetery. Garden hours are sunrise to sunset. Check it out at 325 25 Ave SE, or phone (403) 245-3252.*

On a hot afternoon there's no better place to go people watching than 17th Ave where the young and not-so-young flock to see and be seen. The 12-block stretch of cool stores, restaurants and pub patios was dubbed the Red Mile during those halcyon days of 2004 when the Calgary Flames hockey team made a successful seven-game run for the Stanley Cup. Thousands gathered nightly on the street to celebrate and be merry.

One of the things that make the street so attractive in a town dominated by malls and franchises is its collection of independent boutiques and eateries set in one of Calgary's oldest neighbourhoods. Among the 450-odd shops and services is an eclectic mix of uptown chic-and-pricey stores like Buhran, where you can buy a piece of Afghan architectural history, and reasonably priced Rockabilly clothing at Blame Betty.

In between you'll find ethnic, fashionable and greasy-spoon fare, book and bead stores, luxury spas, sports bars, Calgary's favourite fetish stop – the B&D Emporium, and the ubiquitous Ship and Anchor pub. The Ship, on 5th Street and 17th Ave, has hosted visiting rock stars and actors in its cool, dark interior where attractive clientele can quaff suds from western Canada's largest selection of draught beer. It boasts two large patios, live music, the best fries in town, and a surprisingly relaxed atmosphere where suits to dreads mix and sometimes even court. Get there early, though, because line-ups are common.

Details: *17th Ave runs east to west and is most fun between 14th Street SW and 2nd Street SW.*

Kilts and Sporrans   73

There's something about men in full Scottish dress – the kilt and jacket and sporran. They stand different and, let's face it, walk different with the pleats swirling around their knees. For those of us who don't have the full regalia (or even part of the regalia) stored away at home but want to feel bonny, the Highland Scottish Gift Shoppe is the place to go to rent some Scottish flavour.

The family-run business has been around since 1975 and offers everything Scottish from formal highland kilt rentals, including sgian dubhs (ceremonial knives), and natty ghillie brogues, to bagpipes, smallpipes, whistles and bodhrans. They will even help you plan a

Celtic wedding, sell you a ring, make a customized kilt in your clan tartan, and suggest a piper to boot.

Calgarians in particular seem to grab on to every opportunity they can to bring out the kilts and pipes. Witness Calgary MLA Wayne Cao, a Vietnamese immigrant, belting out the national anthem endearingly off-key and dressed in a kilt. And where else - outside of the misty land itself - would you see a holy Jewish scripture being heralded by a kilt-wearing guy playing a bagpipe en route to its new abode in an orthodox synagogue?

Southern Alberta is infused with Scottish influence, from place names like Airdrie and Banff, to last names (there are two full pages of Campbells in the Calgary phone book). Canmore's Highland Games over the Labour Day weekend has become one of the largest in western Canada, attracting burly caber tossers and bonny lassies alike. And both wear kilts.

Details: *The Highland Shoppe is located at 390, 85 Street SW, directly east of Canada Olympic Park ski jump off the TransCanada Highway. Call (403) 286-1932 or check it out online at www.highlandshoppe.ab.ca.*

Central

LEGEND / L...GENDE

○ Provincial capital /
   Capitale provinciale

· Other populated places /
   Autres lieux habitÈs

—⊕— Trans-Canada Highway /
    La Transcanadienne

——— Major road /
    Route principale

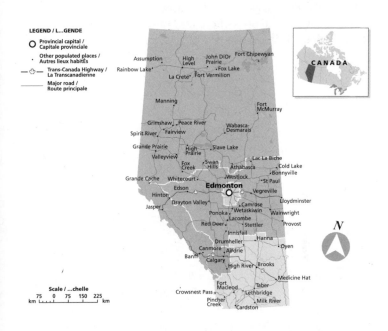

CANADA

N

Scale / ...chelle
75   0   75   150   225
km └┴┴┴┴┴┴┘ km

74   Clifford E. Lee Sanctuary

Twitchers and wildlife enthusiasts alike will enjoy this meander along a gentle marsh less than an hour southeast of Edmonton at the Clifford E. Lee Nature Sanctuary. Armed with mosquito repellant, patience, and a good reference book, people of all ages and physical abilities can spot some of the more than 100 species of our feathered friends visiting the sanctuary.

You might flush out a ring-necked pheasant or ruffed grouse, see black terns and red-winged blackbirds swoop for bugs, hear the knock-knock of woodpeckers or watch northern harriers and red-tailed hawks on the hunt.

A kilometre of boardwalk and five kilometers of connected wide trails (like the 2 kilometre woodland flower walk) take you through marshes, sand hills, meadows and aspen and pine woods on well-marked loops even big Uncle Bill can maneuver. There are benches along most of the way, too, for quick or lengthy sit-downs.

This unassuming little gem, part of Alberta's six designated "Special Places" (code for "pretty but not protected"), also supports animals like deer, coyotes and splashy beaver and muskrat. It is festooned with wildflowers from May to August, some of which are identified by interpretive signboards located throughout the sanctuary by Fish and Wildlife Services.

TAKE 5 GAIL HALL
A FARMERS' MARKET MUST LIST

Edmonton culinarian and food activist, Gail Hall is passionate about food. She confesses that her food apprenticeship began at the age of 5, helping her mother shop for groceries and cook for their family of five. She loved the attention and gratification feeding people fresh wholesome food gave her. For 18 years the face of catering changed dramatically in Edmonton through Gail's customized full-service catering company, Gourmet Goodies. Garnering multiple business awards, it grew to become one of the largest catering operations in Canada, employing 80 full and part time staff and generating over $3 million annually. Gail now owns and operates Seasoned Solutions Loft Cooking School and Culinary Tours, a business that satisfies her passion for sourcing local and regional ingredients, supporting the local agricultural community and promoting the social and cultural importance of cooking and eating well. Below is her must list of farmers' markets found around the province.

1. **The City Market downtown on 104th** is one of the oldest markets in the province and has been part of Edmonton's downtown culture for more than a century. Since 2003, this market is now outdoors and has a great mix of farm fresh produce, baking, fashions and accessories. And it just happens to be on the same street as my Loft Cooking School. Students shop the market with me, meet vendors and purchase ingredients, which they then create into a scrumptious three-course meal, paired with Canadian wines.

Details: *From Edmonton take Highway 16 east (to Jasper), turn south (left) onto Highway 60 (to Devon) and drive 13.2 kilometres. Turn right onto Woodbend Road and drive 1.6 kilometres. Turn south (left) on Range Road 264 and proceed 1.4 kilometres, and turn right into the sanctuary parking area. For further information call Ducks Unlimited at (866) 479-3825.*

2. **The Salisbury Greenhouse in Sherwood Park** is a perfect marriage of greenhouse surroundings and farmers' market vendors. This indoor market operates throughout the winter. Not only can you shop for farm fresh produce and products, but you're automatically exposed to the mind and health benefits of the greenhouse when all is white outside!

3. **The St. Albert Farmers' Market** has the distinction of being the largest farmers' market in western Canada. It is located outdoors in the heart of downtown St. Albert, just north of Edmonton, where over 250 vendors wind their way along downtown streets.

4. My favourite country market is the **Millarville Farmers' Market in southern Alberta**. It's the largest outdoor market in that part of the province and although it has grown from six original vendors to over 170 today, it hasn't lost that country feel that you experience when shopping at a market in the countryside.

5. **The Calgary Farmers' Market in the Curry Barracks** is my favourite year round indoor market. It's everything that an indoor farmers' market should be; large, airy, busy, bustling with a cooperative sense of community. It's not unusual to spend the better part of the day at this market, sampling foods, purchasing breakfast or lunch and taking in the entertainment.

When I was a kid, my dad and I would sometimes sit and sing railway songs together, him playing the guitar in a finger-picking country folk style and me warbling earnestly along. Dad's gone now, but the love of trains has remained. Alberta Prairie Railway Excursions offers a quick and kitschy fix for train buffs involving bandits, Metis heroes and (again with the singing) dinner theatre.

Starting in Stettler, about an hour and a half due east of Red Deer, you'll ride in vintage passenger coaches pulled by a 1920 Baldwin steam engine or a 1950s 1200 series diesel-powered locomotive for a five- to seven-hour journey.

The trip takes you through rolling hills and lush farmland to the village of Big Valley, with the costumed crew providing entertainment. Don't tell the kids, but depending on which excursion you choose during the summer the gun-totin', horse-riding Bolton Band might make the train come to a screeching halt while they board and try to shake down the passengers. It's hokey and hilarious and you never really know when it's going to happen until it does – how fun is that?

By mid afternoon you pull in to the town of Big Valley where you can explore the restored 1912 Canadian Northern Railway station and other historic sites before having a home-style dinner at the community hall.

Details: *From May to mid-October the company offers a variety of country dinner specials, murder mysteries, a family special, live theatre and the ever-popular Teddy Bear special. In the winter hop on for a fine dining railway experience, with a five-course meal plus entertainment. For more information call (403) 742-2811 in Stettler, or (403) 290-0980 in Calgary, or log on to www.absteamtrain.com.*

TAKE 5 TOM TAIT
A PUBLISHER'S MUST LIST

Tom Tait had an Alberta beginning; born in Red Deer and educated up to first year university in Calgary in 1960. But he was soon travelling the world; the next 15 years involved stints in Ottawa interspersed with postings in Paris and Kinshasa as a member of the Canadian Foreign Service, and later in Switzerland with a private company working primarily in North Africa. The entrepreneurial spirit of Alberta drew him back to Calgary and he became the founding publisher of *WHERE Calgary* magazine in 1981. Tom sold his interest in the magazine in 2001, then a year later launched *Galleries West*, a magazine about the visual arts in western Canada. He continues to publish it from Calgary, where he and wife Sandra live downtown in the middle of their favourite city.

1. My favourite thing about Alberta is the ever-changing weather and the way, when you look out to the west, the sky and light are constantly changing. We have the most incredible light here. There is no end to subject matter for artists because the subject changes so dramatically over the course of a day.

2. Something else that's terrific in our province is the good state of the roads. I have the same Alfa Romeo I bought in Paris in 1967 and to take it out on Highway 22 and drive along the eastern slopes of the Rockies on a summer evening at dusk is magical – especially if there is a full moon hanging low over the mountains.

3. We also are so blessed with golf courses in general, and in particular the public courses in Kananaskis. But there is a new course, the Sirocco, just four kilometres south of Spruce Meadows on the outskirts of Calgary that is a recent favourite. And to golf there isn't financially outrageous.

4. I have a particular affection for Waterton. People are there for no particular reason – they're not on their way somewhere else, they're just stopping in. It's more laid back than other mountain towns like Banff. And Parks Canada made a conscious decision not to expand, keeping it about the same size as 50 years ago.

5. For me, the real jewel is Prince's Island, near where I live. It's always a pleasant walk and it has so much going for it in a tiny space, from music and cultural festivals, to Shakespeare-in-the-Park, to fine dining. The wetlands area on the east end is home to a beaver which came back after being trapped and transported 100 kilometres away for chewing down a substantial amount of trees by the park. Park managers figure it deserves to stay, and are keeping an eye on it.

For those with deep pockets, Canadian Pacific Railways offers an amazing six day/five night tour of the Rockies or fly fishing adventure on its luxury train starting (and ending) in Calgary. If the $8,000 price tag isn't a problem, but time's a constraint, you can still book the revamped railcars for a private dinner trip to Banff and back, avec beaucoup des cocktails et hors d'oeuvres, for an undisclosed sum. Discrete enquiries can be directed to (403) 508-1400.

76 | Alberta Sports Hall of Fame

The Alberta Sports Hall of Fame and Museum is a fun stop for the restless hockey or baseball nut in the family if you're traveling west of Red Deer on the Queen E Highway. The 7,000 square-foot facility honours players and developers of the iconic Canadian game, as well as other sports figureheads. There are more than 7,000 pieces of sports paraphernalia in the hall, including photos, jerseys and awards.

Most kids will scoot through the exhibits of sports paraphernalia to get to the important stuff - the games. Because it is all about the game, the computerized interactive game. Try your hand at pitching a baseball, throwing the pigskin deep, taking shots on a goalie, shooting hoops or kicking a soccer goal in the multisport virtual systems area.

There's a circulating climbing wall for the little monkeys, a three-hole putting green and the unusual addition of a 200-meter wheelchair challenge. It's an eye-opener to strap yourself in a sports wheelchair and "race" against a friend or a staff member on a computerized screen.

The Ice and Snow exhibit is a tad bare, but has an alpine ski racer game to pick up the speed.

When it's time to call a time out, the 40-seat theatre is a good place to catch your breath while watching surprisingly interesting presentations of past sports highlights and personalities.

Details: *#30 Riverview Park, Red Deer – just off Highway 2, north of the 32nd Street overpass. Call (403) 341-8614 or check out www.albertasportshalloffame.com.*

No Pigeons in this Pie 77

The owners of ECO Café in Pigeon Lake were thinking globally and acting locally way before the 100-mile diet shot into the spotlight. Known as one of Alberta's hidden culinary treasures, Tim and Deb Wood have made buying local meat, fowl and produce, organic when possible, for  their dishes a priority since 1982 "because it's the right thing to do," the uber-driven couple say.

The café might easily be mistaken for one of those nice but bland restaurants often seen in small communities like the Village at Pigeon Lake, population 400. That is until you step inside and look at the menu, which highlights what Chef Tim characterizes as world food. The selection is weighted toward carnivores, with Asian, Mediterranean, Moroccan and new Canadian cuisine showcased on the plate.

Chef Tim's signature piece and one people come back for time and again is the game-meat pie, a delectable dish made with locally sourced duck, pork and elk. The wild boar stew served with organic veggies over pasta is another favourite.

The recently updated café is spacious and bright, with ochre ceilings and floor, a sinuous birch beverage bar, a bold natural gas fireplace, recessed lighting in the high ceiling and a slightly Zen oriental tone to its décor. Compost bins in the back and cornstarch-based takeout containers also show the Wood's commitment to reducing their environmental footprint.

Details: *The ECO Café caters to locals and opens daily at 6:30 am, closing between 8 pm and 9 pm. It is located directly west of Wetaskiwin on Highway 13, turning off the Queen Elizabeth Highway. Phone (780) 586-2627, or log on to www.ecocafepigeonlake.ca.*

78 Red Deer

The third biggest city in Alberta sits among rolling hills, grain farms, ranches and a whole bunch of oil field service industries. Red Deer's origins as a stopping point between Edmonton to the north and Calgary to the south persist to today par-

ticularly since the city of 85,000 is bisected by the Queen Elizabeth Highway, also known as the Queen E, or Highway 2.

The stretch known as Gasoline Alley where truckers and travellers pump up and get out is unremarkable in the food and retail choices available, so head to Alexander Way inside the city. The small but vibrant pedestrian section of downtown hosts funky stores, cheeky street art and indie eateries. The 48 Street promenade also is close to historic buildings such as the old Armoury and CPR railway station.

On the east end of town, make a pilgrimage to St. Mary's Church, an astoundingly beautiful modern structure designed by homeboy and world-acclaimed architect Douglas Cardinal in 1968. The entire brick building is curved, from walls to roofline, presenting an organic, sinuous presence on the otherwise bland prairie landscape. Cardinal is famous for his flowing architecture that borrows from his Metis heritage and European expressionism.

West of the city, make a stop at the historic Fort Normandeau Interpretive Centre on Highway 2. Before the iron horse came and Red Deer became a town, it was a stopping house right at the best river crossing site for miles that had been used by Aboriginals and bison for hundreds of years. Interpreters and displays at the charming site tell the stories of the Cree and Blackfoot people, the Metis and early Europeans who settled in the area.

Details: *The church is on the corner of 38 St and Mitchell Ave and is open to visitors weekdays from 10 am – 4 pm. Call 403-347-3114 for more information.*

Rocky Mountain House Light Show 79

If you get a chance to fly over Rocky Mountain House during December, say between Edmonton and Vancouver, make sure it's after dark, and then look out the window. Beaming up with good cheer and about 75,000 Christmas lights is Alfred and Cheryl Von Hollen's house, a sight passengers cruising at 30,000 feet can see below.

Arguably the most famous home in the town of 6,500, the two-story home is bedecked and festooned with lights, ribbons and boughs, stars and holiday symbols from top to bottom. But there's much more than a light show to enjoy; it's walking around the property that's really fun, even when it's bone-chillingly cold: Alfred sets up more than 30 inflatable lawn ornaments, including a Santa popping out of an igloo and snow globes, plus has dozens of animated figures, toys, animals and trains, as well as – of course – carols in the background.

The decorations are sweetly tacky and the spirit is as animated as the reindeer, making it easy to enjoy the good cheer. There's so much to gawk at and comment about that even teens could enjoy a walk through.

Details: *From the first week of December to January 1, several thousand people make the trek on Highway 11 to the bright, flashing home. Bring a donation to the food bank when you do, and check out www.rockymtnhouse.com to see when the Von Hollen's are having their one-day open house fundraiser. Inside the couple have eight themed trees, three equally adorable miniature villages and 70 nativity scenes. To get to the Von Hollen home, head west on Highway 11 into Rocky Mountain House, turn left on 57th Avenue and turn right on 57th Street Close.*

South East

LEGEND / L...GENDE

O Provincial capital /
  Capitale provinciale

. Other populated places /
  Autres lieux habitÉs

— ⌂ — Trans-Canada Highway /
  La Transcanadienne

___ Major road /
  Route principale

CANADA

N

Scale / ...chelle
75 0 75 150 225
km |.....|.....| km

Fort Chipewyan
John DiOr
Prairie
Assumption
High Level
Fox Lake
Rainbow Lake
La Crete Fort Vermilion
Manning
Fort McMurray
Grimshaw Peace River
Wabasca-Desmarais
Spirit River Fairview
Grande Prairie High Prairie Slave Lake
Valleyview
Fox Creek Swan Hills Lac La Biche
Athabasca Cold Lake
Bonnyville
Grande Cache Whitecourt Westlock St Paul
Edson **Edmonton** Vegreville
Hinton Drayton Valley Lloydminster
Jasper Camrose Wetaskiwin Wainwright
Ponoka Lacombe
Red Deer Stettler Provost
Innisfail
Drumheller Hanna
Canmore Airdrie Oyen
Banff Calgary
High River Brooks
Medicine Hat
Fort Macleod Taber
Crowsnest Pass Lethbridge
Pincher Creek Milk River
Cardston

---

80   To Evolve or Not

Here's an interesting he said-she said sort of day trip: Drive out to the Royal Tyrell Museum just outside of the southern Alberta town of Drumheller and spend the morning wandering around fascinating exhibits about life millions of years ago, dinosaur bones included. Walk through a recreation of Burgess Shale, now a mountain ridge in Yoho National Park, where 140 species of soft-bodied organisms swam more than 500 million years ago. Or watch a recreation of a 375-million-year-old reef environment with thousands of life-like models showing what Alberta was like underwater.

In 2009 you might even take part in celebrating the 150 years of Charles Darwin's "On the Origin of the Species," the tome on evolution that changed the world of science. Then after lunch, motor up Highway 56 another 60 kilometers north to the village of Big Valley and Canada's first permanent creationist museum.

Housed in a slightly more modest facility than the 11,000-square-foot Tyrell, the Big Valley Creation Science Museum was built to "refute the lie of evolution." Included among its equally fascinating fossils and exhibits in the revamped bungalow is a giant model of

Noah's ark in the "Dinosaurs and the Flood" display, and another display showing considerable evidence that humans and dinosaurs coexisted.

Kids can enjoy several interactive displays, as well as the numerous fossils and recreations of dinosaurs.

Details: *The Big Valley Creationist Museum is closed during the winter, but if you call (403) 876-2100 or email info@bvcsm.com, owner Harry Nibourg might be able to open the facility for you. Big Valley is 32 kilometers south of Stettler on Highway 56, or 62 kilometres north of Drumheller on the same highway. Drumheller is almost two hours northeast of Calgary taking Highway 2 north, then east along Highway 72, and then Highway 9.*

Gopher Hole Museum 81

Call me crazy, but I think no road trip in southern Alberta is complete without a visit to the Gopher Hole Museum in Torrington. Those of us who enjoy the weird thank this village of 210 people that apologizes to no one for its politically incorrect displays of stuffed Richardson ground squirrels.

For $2 an adult and 50 cents a kid, you experience typical (gopher) Torrington village life, from the fru-fru beauty salon with the hairdresser exclaiming, "I'm a beautician, not a magician!" to the church scene where the reverend preaches to a sleeping congregant while an angel dangles in the background.

Each one of the 77 gophers in the 41 anthropomorphic displays is dressed in outfits hand-stitched by locals. Two retired carpenters built the cabinets and a local artist painted the backdrops to the town dioramas they inhabit.

The museum rises above being just strange by the sense of whimsy which shows a delightful lack of self-conceit on the part of village. Just don't expect any famous people being depicted, museum director Dianne Kurta says.

Since opening in 1996, the museum has garnered lots of publicity, especially after People for the Ethical Treatment of Animals caught wind of the project. Their letters and those of others protesting the displays are available for visitors to read.

The museum has captured such a wide audience, it has been requested to contribute a diorama to a taxidermy display for the 2010 Olympics in British Columbia. About 5,000 people tour the Gopher Hole between June and the end of September. The museum is open from 10 am to 5 pm daily. During the off season, call the number on the museum door, and someone will open it up for you.

Details: *From Highway 2, turn due east at Olds onto Highway 27 and follow the signs. The Gopher Hole Museum is located at 208 1 St S, Torrington. Or call (403) 631-2133 for more information.*

82   Medicine Hat's a Gas

Someone once characterized Medicine Hat as being one of the few places in the world where saying, "I think I smell gas," was a matter of civic pride.

"All hell for a basement," 19th century author Rudyard Kipling said of the city, which sits atop a huge natural gas field and has the only municipal utility in Canada to own its own source of heat and electricity.

The Hat also is Canada's sunniest and Alberta's driest town, making the flourishing city of 60,000 a retirement haven with some (seven within city limits) really (and I mean really) nice golf courses. The semi-arid climate also attracts black widow spiders, scorpions and rattlesnakes, so, going barefoot usually is discouraged in parts of town. It also is a surprising hotbed of arts and music, hosting the province's third largest jazz festival each year and a number of arts-related events springing from the Medicine Hat College and local writers and artists.

The 60,000-square-foot Esplanade Arts and Heritage Centre contrasts the river valley with steel and concrete architecture which encases a 700-seat theatre, the museum, discovery centre, studio theatre and galleries for fine arts and traveling exhibitions.

Downtown is picturesque, with 277 gas street lamps burning

night and day and many more interesting shops than uptown where the big box stores are. Ignore the franchise coffee shops and take a break at the Madhatter Coffee Roastery for the best cuppa joe in town.

Paddling along the lazy river is a delightful way of experiencing the local landscapes, and staff at Police Point Park Nature Centre are happy to organize a tour. These folks have some fabulous off-the-beaten-track packages that include river canoeing during the day and sleeping in a tipi at night, exploring nearby Cypress Hills, or touring ghost towns and old cemeteries.

TAKE 5 DIANE WILD
FIVE MOTORCYCLE RIDE MUSTS

Diane Wild was proudly born and raised and spent most of her life in Calgary. Hobbies include motorcycling, gardening, cooking, traveling, fishing, and being a perpetual university student. She dreams of motorcycle trips in Canada, Australia and Europe, fishing off Port Hardy, B.C., and quiet time in a cottage in Italy, Australia or Whitehorse. For excitement she works in the motorcycle industry and plans motorcycle trips for customers.

1. Ride from Calgary northeast to Rosebud in August on the back roads of the Highways 564 and 840. There is nothing more relaxing than the sights and smells of the Prairies just before harvest along sweeping, quiet roads. As you ride along the rolling hills, you'll see yellow and blue fields flowing like gentle waves and smell their sweetness. Finally the road starts to twist just a little as you approach the Badlands area and into Rosebud. Take time to visit the museum, and attend a play at their live theatre.

2. Ride from Calgary due south to Waterton National Park, taking Highways 22 (Cowboy Trail) and 6. Here you are able to keep the weather-volatile Rockies off to your right and miss the storms that usually brew up. Instead, it is sunny and hot and the ever-turning highway lulls you into a state of hypnosis as you lean to the right and then to the left. At the end of Highway 22, take a jog onto Highway 6 which is in the windy end of the province, as evidenced by the huge wind turbine farms. The jewel is, once you get through the winds, Waterton Park is tucked into the mountains on the lakeside.

Calaway Park 83

Chaos! Cosmic Spins! Plummeting 40 feet in free-fall fancy, wondering why the heck you took the bet! Adrenalin junkies of all ages can get their thrills at Calaway Park, a 160-acre ride and entertainment emporium just five minutes west of Calgary on Highway #1.

Calaway Park is western Canada's largest outdoor amusement park, with 33 rides to choose from, a multitude of food vendors and shows

3. Ride the David Thompson Highway (Highway 11) east from Saskatchewan River Crossing in Banff National Park to Nordegg and then onto Rocky Mountain House. The most vivid colours of spruce and pine green forests to your left, blue waters of the lake to your right and black clouds straight ahead make this road memorable. Its proximity to the Rockies almost always means you will ride into a rain or hail storm!

4. Ride the Highwood Pass (Highway 40) when open between June 16 and November 30. The pass is 2,206 metres high and places you in the middle of the rough, craggy, confining Rocky Mountains with lots of wildlife (and some not so wild cows) and temperature drops of 25 degrees C. How the scenery can change from flat prairie to bold, sharp mountains! It is THE most popular Sunday ride for Calgary motorcyclists. Take a picnic lunch with you.

5. Ride to Fort Macleod and Head-Smashed-In Buffalo Jump along Highway 24/23 via Carseland and Vulcan. Looking for the roads less traveled and trying to stay out of the winds, this road is quiet and unassuming but watch out for at-grade railroad tracks. The hot plains mean on a sunny summer day you can encounter heat riding a motorcycle that won't cool – you can feel it coming right back at you from the engine.

on the grounds to take in when you've had enough of being thrown around by a mechanical tea cup.

Day and season passes are affordable, the rides are varied and enough to keep the entire family amused, terrified or wet, depending on your choice.

A traditional summer vacation destination for families throughout southern Alberta and into Saskatchewan, the park reinvented itself from a sleepy, kinda ho-hum western theme park with Hanna Barbara characters in the 1980s and 1990s to its current mix of soft kiddie rides like the Tot Yachts to the terrifyingly cool Vortex corkscrew roller coaster. The little guys can practice their driving skills with bumper cars and boats, or ride a junior version of a roller coaster.

For those of us who want a gasp of excitement without losing their lunch, the Dream Machine is a swinging ride that gives a bit of bragging rights. And very little beats the Shoot the Chutes ride on a hot day, when you zoom down a stomach-clenching slide to drop into a picturesque pond.

Like any amusement park, expect line-ups to favourite rides during the height of the season. Late spring and post-Stampede in late July, when both Calgarians and tourists have had their thrills, are good times to avoid crowds. But sometimes the crowds are part of the attraction, along with the cotton candy and admonitions to buckle up and hold on tight!

Details: *Open weekends mid-May to mid-June, daily late June to end of August, weekends only September to October. Five minutes out of the west end of Calgary on Highway 1. The exit for Calaway Park is exit 169 and called Springbank Road. There are signs for Calaway Park before the turn.*

84 Windmill Central

Tilting at windmills tends to be a provincial sport in southwestern Alberta, which boasts the second largest concentration of wind farms in Canada, after Ontario. But long before the elegant white towers of electrical power were created, wooden windmills spun their wheels and vanes across the Prairies to bring water to thirsty homesteaders.

The tiny hamlet (population 30) of Etzikom (Blackfoot for 'coulee') honors the tradition with Canada's Historic Windmill Interpretive Centre, adjacent to its Heritage Museum. The 14 restored windmills at the centre include a replica of a European postmill as well as old farm windmills. They don't take long to tour, so definitely take a dip into the Heritage Museum (which also is the only place in town to get a snack).

Interestingly, Etzikom is part of the County of Forty Miles' Ghost Town tours, which makes museum curator Pear Brower, whose family has ranched in the region for five generations, exclaim "there aren't that many of us left, but we're definitely not ghosts." The museum recreates an old time prairie Main Street, complete with blacksmith shop, general store, hotel and school house, all within the gymnasium of the hamlet's school.

Details: *Take Highway 61 east of Foremost for 10 kilometres. It's open 10 am to 5 pm Monday to Friday. Museum telephone: (403) 666-3915 or 3792.*

Cypress Hills 85

The Cypress Hills in south eastern Alberta offer a cool refuge from blistering hot prairie summers and serene skiing or snowshoeing during the winter. The ancient plateau of hills rises more than 600 metres from the semi-arid plains and are the highest point in Canada between the Rockies and Labrador (1,466 metres), are rich with wildlife and vegetation, and are the site of human habitation for millenniums.

I first discovered the charms of Cypress Hills during a stint in Medicine Hat, driving 65 kilometres down Highway 41 on a sticky summer Saturday with a crew of friends desperate to throw ourselves into the cool (and crowded) Elkwater Lake. Later that year I hiked the trails snaking through Cypress Hills Interprovincial Park and that winter learned how to cross-country ski up in the Hidden Valley ski area.

The hamlet of Elkwater sits at the same elevation as Banff at

1,233 metres and caters to a brisk tourism trade (both summer and winter) but is more limited in conveniences. There are plenty of campsites, plus the more upscale Elkwater Lodge and Resort and Bar-Zee Bed & Breakfast.

Aboriginal people have hunted and camped here for at least 7,000 years, according to archeological finds. The region also was the site of the Cypress Hills Massacre in 1873, a tragic event that led to the creation of the North West Mounted Police. You can visit the Fort Walsh National Historic Site and reconstructed whiskey trading post in the park. After playing around, drive up the highway to the viewpoint at the southern border of the park. Get out of the car and spend a few minutes looking at one of the most sweeping vistas in the country.

Details: *More information can be found about Cypress Hills Interprovincial Park by calling (403) 893-3833, or going online at www.cypresshills.com.*

86 Hog Wild

Seven Persons was originally founded by Cyrl Ogston after he fled the unsympathetic United States in search of a place where he, a devout Mormon, could practice polygamy. Nowadays, more Mennonites live in the hamlet of 250, which got its name either from a railroad construction crew in the late 1800s which found seven rough graves or from a battle between Blood Indians and Cree that resulted in seven deaths.

Wherever the name came from, this is sausage country. Devotees from as far as Calgary (some 300 kilometres north) make the trek to the hamlet for Ralph and Elaine Erb's tasty sausages of naturally-raised pork, as well as beef sausages and a pork/elk combination. "I'd say 75 percent of the sausage goes on the highway," Ralph says, meaning people make a special trip.

Their shop, Premium Sausage, just off Highway 3, is seeped in European atmosphere and reminiscent of meat markets found in Germany. (Ralph is from Waterloo County in Ontario.) He came to Alberta back in the early 1970s with a buddy and wound up farming in the region. His European-style homemade sausage proved so popular, he quit farming and set up shop in 1990. "This business is way better," he says, wrapping a smaller order for a local resident.

Details: *To get there from Medicine Hat take Highway 3 west for 10 kilometres, or 70 kilometres east from Taber. For more information, call (403) 832-2224 or log onto www.premiumsausage.ca.*

Red Rock Coulee 87

After having a nosh in Seven Persons, turn south on Highway 877 for about 15 minutes for another provincial anomaly, the stark and somewhat bizarre Alberta natural site, Red Rock Coulee. Like the remnants of a giant game of bocci ball, the massive sandstone concretions of Red Rock Coulee lie strewn about on the bottom of the Bearpaw Sea, dry now for millions of years.

Millenniums of erosion and pressure left the giant rusty-coloured boulders, some of the largest in the world, which actually grew from an iron oxide-secreting bacteria colony. Check out the rock surfaces and you might see the fossilized remains of oysters, clams, fish scales and occasionally, broken dinosaur or turtle bones.

Red Rock Coulee spans 324 hectares and, despite being brittle-dry in the summer, supports a variety of wildlife. Jackrabbits, mule deer, the graceful pronghorn and numerous birds can all be found there. If you're lucky, an eastern short-horned lizard might run across your path.

A word of caution – don't go lifting any rocks; rattlesnakes, venomous spiders and scorpions also live in the coulee, which turns mighty slippery when wet since it is made of bentonitic soil, or clay. There are picnic tables to set up a lunch or dinner, and pit toilets, but no concessions so bring your own food and beverages.

Details: *To get there, make your way to Highway 3, also known as the Crowsnest Highway that exits Medicine Hat to the west. At Seven Persons, turn south on Highway 887 for 25 kilometres to the gravel road access to Red Rock Coulee.*

88   Rock On

Remember that scene in *Mission Impossible* when Tom Cruise's character is hanging off a cliff by his fingernails? You can be just like him, rock climbing in Kananaskis Country an hour west of Calgary. Okay, maybe not just like Cruise, but with some instruction in the city, a few bucks worth of rental equipment and a good guide, you and your kids can scale a rock face, and – most importantly – live to brag the tale.

Start off at the University of Calgary which offers both classes for newbies and rentals of such essential equipment as harness, helmet and chalk bag. Together with the university and Yamnuska Mountain Adventures, beginner climbers are taken to simple rock climbs like Wasootch Slabs in Kananaskis Country, a 4,211-square-kilometre tract of land straddling the foothills and the Rockies.

For those of us who prefer a little less adrenalin, the U of C indoor climbing wall is almost like the real thing. The 40-foot slab of concrete is the only one of its kind in the city, embedded with real quartzite set at different angles with overhangs, artificial holds, vertical and horizontal cracks, those essential finger holds and the mysterious friction bulges. It was designed for teaching rock climbing and mountaineering skills and its climbing surfaces are designed for landing on gear, anchor building and rappelling. Instructors can also simulate conditions for rock and crevasse rescue.

Details: *For more information, contact the University of Calgary Outdoor Centre at 250 University Drive; tel: (403) 220-503; web: www.calgaryoutdoorcentre.ca/climbing.*

Horseshoe Canyon | 89

A perennial favourite in the easy hiking roster of southern Alberta is Horseshoe Canyon in the Red Deer River Badlands, near Drumheller.

Shaped like its name, the canyon runs three kilometres through prime fossil country and has a number of fairly easy walking trails, which are accessed after you climb down 60 metres into a wide, grassy area; so some degree of mobility is required. Within a few minutes the main trail narrows and starts twisting as befitting a canyon carved out by seasonal water flows, eventually leading to clay hoodoo formations.

Along the way there are small creeks, hills, plateaus and a variety

of plants and animals to watch (and watch out for) while admiring the walls of the canyon. The different ribbons of colours and shapes, pits and caves throughout the site are full of mystery and history, resulting from millenniums of water and wind.

The best time of year to visit Horseshoe Canyon is in the late spring when the flowers are still out, the floor of the canyon isn't too wet, and it's not baking hot. By mid-June it is typical sizzling badland terrain, so take lots of water and sunscreen, plus wear a hat – Alberta sun is piercing. And keep a sharp eye out for snakes. If aerial travel is more your style, helicopter rides usually are available for a reasonable rate during the season.

Details: *Horseshoe Canyon recreation area is located on Highway 9, 17 kilometers south west of Drumheller, and about an hour and a half northeast of Calgary. There are bathrooms at the entrance to the canyon and a miracle of an ice cream shop which also sells pop and coffee. Call (403) 823-1749 for more information.*

90   Ba-Ba Brunch

Mother's Day brunch buffet at PaSu Farm is a well-loved tradition for those who know enough to make reservations for the popular eatery and working farm northwest of Calgary. A typical visit involves scrumptious lamb dishes (although other meat and fowl are served), market greens, an outstanding view of the Rockies and maybe a little shopping for sheepskin slippers or a mohair wrap afterwards.

PaSu was started by South Africans Patrick and Susan (guess where the farm's name came from) de Rosemond in 1977 and grew to include a European country restaurant and boutique. Patrick, a foodie from way back, became the chef in 1995 after hiring a series of strange and unreliable cooks and often quotes Harriet Van Horne saying, "Cooking is like love. It should be entered into with abandon or not at all."

He's instituted the wildly successful adult-only Valentine's erotic gourmet evening, and the seven course plate service Fine Dining series, among other events. You might see him walking about with his cockatoo Peaches (definitely not on the menu) after the meal.

In the spring, the kiddies will have fun watching the little lamb-sies, but my advice would be to go outside AFTER the meal.

Details: *Go north from Calgary on the Queen Elizabeth Highway (Highway 2) for about 45 minutes. The farm is off Secondary Highway 580, and there are signs on Highway 2, Highway 2A and at every intersection leading to PaSu Farm. Call toll-free (800) 679-7999, locally at (403) 337-2800, or on the web at www.pasu.com.*

South West

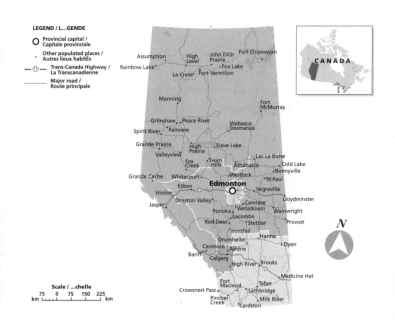

LEGEND / L...GENDE

○ Provincial capital / Capitale provinciale

· Other populated places / Autres lieux habitÉs

— 🍁 — Trans-Canada Highway / La Transcanadienne

—— Major road / Route principale

CANADA

N

Scale / ...chelle
75 0 75 150 225
km └┴┴┴┘   km

Dinosaur Provincial Park   91

Coming up to Dinosaur Provincial Park is like suddenly landing on the moon. One minute you're driving along the Prairies surrounded by flat grasslands, the next – shazam! An enormous crater opens in front of you, full of eerie formations of sandstone and clay, bizarre hoodoos with roots dating back 75 million years and carved during the last ice age 13,000 years ago.

It is hard to fathom, but sharks and crocodiles once prowled the area and along with them, carnivorous and grass-munching dinos. Protruding from that Bentonire clay is proof that hundreds of such thunder lizards roamed the plain way before the buffalo. The park boasts one of the biggest fossil beds in the world, fossils that continue to literally surface every year, depending on wind and rainfall.

For those of us still using our bones, there's plenty to see at this UNESCO World Heritage Site, so plan to visit for at least a full day. There are bus tours, hiking tours, guided and self-guided trails (two wheelchair accessible) and events, as well as two outdoor display buildings.

I canoed in with a group one summer and stayed at one of the two campgrounds in the park. In the evening we listened to coyotes while watching lightning flash about 60 kilometres away. It's a popular place in the summer time, so best to make a reservation for any of the tours, and definitely the campgrounds.

Details: *Dinosaur Provincial Park is 48 kilometres northeast of Brooks and is accessed from Highways 873 and 544. Call (403) 378-4342 or check out www.dinosaurpark.ca.*

92   Head-Smashed-In Buffalo Jump

It's easy to think you're lost when driving up to Head-Smashed-In Buffalo Jump interpretive centre from the dusty plains outside of Fort Macleod. The UNESCO World Heritage site is built right into the side of the sandstone cliff the jump spills from, melding with the stones, sage and prairie grasses. Head-Smashed-In Buffalo Jump is the oldest, largest and best preserved bison jump in the world, testament to the ingenuity and skill of the peoples that depended on the magnificent animal for their survival.

At the foot of the wind-swept bluff lie the remains of thousands of bison bones, remnants of 5,500 years of continuous use by Plains Indians who herded the bison to the edge of the cliff and to their deaths below. In some places below the jump the bones lie 11 metres deep, and it was there, as legend has it, the body of a young Indian was found, crushed by the beasts he came to see.

The interpretive centre flows up the 10-metre-high cliff side in seven levels that lead you through the ecology, mythology, lifestyle and hunting techniques of Blackfoot peoples. At the top of the centre is the exit to the upper trail viewpoint, a blustery walk to the point where the bison were led off the precipice.

To the west of the cliff are almost 500 cairns lined up for about 14 kilometres toward a fertile area where herds of bison grazed on. Almost six thousand years ago, Plains Indians set up the drive lanes to funnel the animals through to the jump site.

Under the huge prairie sky and as the wind blows down around you from the Porcupine Hills, it's easy to imagine the ground shaking under your feet as hundreds of bison stampede toward their end. There are several jump sites along the cliffs, but the Head-Smashed-In site is the best preserved. There, at the bottom of the jump, the hunters butchered the animals and processed the remains.

Make the stay even more special by spending a night or two

under the stars in a tipi camp in the shadow of the buffalo jump, listening to the legends told by a Blackfoot interpreter. You can be sure the campfire stories will have a lasting impression.

Details: *To get to Head-Smashed-In Buffalo Jump Head, go northwest out of Fort Macleod on Highway 785 for 18 kilometres. Head-Smashed-In Buffalo Jump is open all year except Christmas Eve, Christmas Day, New Year's Day and Easter. Summer and winter hours vary. Call (403) 553-2731 or log onto www.head-smashed-in.com for more information.*

Fort Whoop-Up   93

The lawlessness around this profitable "whisky fort" got so bad its original name of Fort Hamilton was tossed aside for the more representative moniker of Fort Whoop-Up. The debauchery was so prevalent that the fort takes partial credit for the formation of the North West Mounted Police.

Violent clashes, brought on by American traders dealing in contraband liquor and firearms in exchange for furs, prompted the federal government to step in to bring law and order to the west. Thus came about the creation of the NWMP, precursors to the officers in red serge, to protect local aboriginal and settler communities - and secure Canadian sovereignty in the region.

You can explore the fascinating blood-soaked history (that'll get the youngsters' attention) at a loyal recreation of the fort (which was burned down several times) in Indian Battle Park, off the west end of downtown Lethbridge.

Once there, you can explore the two compound buildings and rooms, check out the museum exhibits and learn about making fake whiskey from grain alcohol, spices, molasses and black chewing tobacco. Throughout the year there are events such as gun fights during Dominion Day (beats the pony rides any day) and Christmas at the Fort.

The park where the fort is located is marked to the north by the soaring High Level Bridge, the tallest railway bridge in the world at 97 metres, and stretching 1.6 kilometres across the Oldman River.

Indian Battle Park lies in the river valley surrounded by coulees rising 300 feet from prairie level to floodplain. As its name indicates, it was the site of the last great battle between the Cree and Blackfoot nations in 1870. The two tribes still have chest thumping contests, but generally are more jovial than warrior-like.

Details: *In Lethbridge, turn west towards the river on 3 Ave South from Scenic Drive South. Open all year. Call (403)329-0444 or check out www.fortwhoopup.com.*

94   Full Moon Craziness in June

Ever get that feeling you just want to chuck it all for a chance to mountain bike, trek in the forest with no GPS, paddle white water rapids and climb up a rock face – all in 36 hours as part of a team? Apparently dozens of hard-core adventure racers do, and up to 160 of them take part in the grueling Full Moon in June event each year.

Run by Brian Gallant and Andrew Fairhurst, both in Crowsnest Pass, the endurance battle begins under the light of the moon and has teams navigate unmarked trails through mountain passes and along rivers with compasses, maps, altimeters and outdoor know-how.

"I'd say an adventure racer is made up of a third of determination, a third of skill and a third of strength, with a slight dash of insanity to top things off," Gallant says, chuckling. The race is serious business: Most teams have support crews to help them out with the food that's eaten every two hours or so, dry clothing, gear like kayaks, and sundry supplies like bandages – because for adventure racers the rush consists of pushing their limits in the wild, regardless of the finish time or the bruises. And if 36 hours seems a tad long, there's always the eight-hour Half Moon in August.

Details: *Call (403) 563-5766 or check it out on the web at www.fmij.com.*

Writing-on-Stone   95

Writing-on-Stone Provincial Park is one of southern Alberta's magical places, set against dramatic sandstone cliffs, rust-coloured hoodoos and the wide Milk River Valley. For more than 6,000 years, nomadic groups traveled through this fertile, sheltered area, often painting and carving messages to the spirits on the sandstone. The legacy of their travels and spiritual quests live on today in the thousands of pictographs and petroglyphs found in the park, the largest concentration of Native rock art on the North American Plains.

The drawings and carvings of people, animals and events still hold strong spiritual meaning to Blackfoot, many of whom see the site as a sacred place. It is, by any view, a unique combination of carvings – by nature itself in the formation of the bizarre shapes of the hoodoos, and the rock art – cradled by the cliffs and the river valley.

There are several ways to approach the preserve, from the river

TAKE 5 MELLISA HOLLINGSWORTH
A FULL SPEED MUST LIST

Mellisa Hollingsworth, Olympic bronze medalist in the adrenalin-pumping sport of skeleton, is a simple Alberta cowgirl at heart. A fiercely competitive Canadian champion and overall World Cup champion skeleton racer who likes throwing herself on a sled then diving head first down an ice track only to hit speeds up to 140 kilometres an hour, yes, but a cowgirl nonetheless. She's travelled to many continents, including Africa through her volunteer work with Right to Play, and her favourite place, no surprise, is still southern Alberta.

1. I've been so fortunate to have travelled to many different parts of the world with my sport, but every time I land at the Calgary airport a huge sense of relief washes over me. When I fly in and see the mountains to the west and the Prairies stretching out below, I feel that overall sense of home.

2. My parent's ranch is one of my favourite places to be. It is in the foothills near Eckville, where there are big hills, lots of trees and meadows, and where our horses go to pasture. It's amazing to ride through the lush grass in the early evening, with the sun setting in the hills. The view is majestic.

3. Cowboy ranching culture. My parents raised bucking horses and I grew up with rodeo. I enjoy the competitiveness, the work ethic, and the athleticism of the horses and the cowboys on top of them. I have a huge appreciation for the freedom we have in our country and particularly in Alberta, where I have the freedom to slide down an ice track on a skeleton sled or be a barrel racer if I want.

4. I would be remiss if I didn't mention Canada Olympic Park in Calgary. It's a unique attraction and until 2008 had the only skeleton track in Canada. I have to give the facility credit for a large part of our success representing Canada internationally.

5. Family is another big thing I love about Alberta. Most of my family is here - my siblings and parents and friends. And this is where I want to start my own family in the future, after my sports life.

itself by canoe or kayak, walking in from the nearby 64-spot campsite, on a backcountry hike, or walking down to the archeological preserve from two parking lots.

Which ever way you choose, the view is the kind that makes you take in a deep breath and give thanks. You might even catch sight of peregrine falcons, eagles and colourful American kestrels overhead.

Details: *From the town of Milk River, go east of Highway 4 on Highway 501 for 32 kilometres, turn south at the sign Writing-On-Stone Provincial Park for 10 kilometres more. Guided tours are available from May to Labour Day, and the park is open all year. For more information, phone (403) 647-2364.*

96   Mission Church

One of the most romantic places for a wedding has got to be the McDougall Mission Church on the Stoney Reserve. The isolated little white chapel, built in 1875, sits on an open plain overlooking the Bow River, silhouetted by prairie sky and a backdrop of foothills.

The plain Methodist church has been the subject of films (most recently Brad Pitt's *The Assassination of Jessie James*), sentimental television ads, and countless weddings because of its stunning location and quiet, enduring resolve. Surrounded by wild grasses and flowers in the spring, McDougall Church is the second oldest building standing on its original foundations in Alberta. It was restored and made into a provincial heritage site in the 1970s.

An adjacent memorial commemorates its builder, Scottish Reverend George McDougall who lost his way on the prairie during a blizzard in January 1876. His frozen body was found several weeks later. McDougall, a much-trusted mediator for both Stoney and Blackfoot communities, was participating in a buffalo hunt when he got lost.

The church has no congregation now, but is used for weddings, special events and two commemorative services in June and September each year. Take note there is no electricity, water or modern conveniences on site.

Details: *To get there, go west on Highway 1; 27 kilometres west of Cochrane on Highway 1A, 48 kilometres west of Calgary. There is a point of interest sign and a cairn on the highway.*

Bow Valley Provincial Park   97

Often overlooked because of its location on the skirts of grand cousin, Banff National Park, Bow Valley Provincial Park is a less wild

introduction to the Rockies much enjoyed by Calgarians. Set at the confluence of the Bow River and Kananaskis River less than an hour west of town, the park boasts stunning foothill landscapes such as open meadows, forests and rolling hills. All kinds of wildlife wander through its landscape, including deer, moose, the odd bear and even fewer campers meandering through the area from one of two electricity-and-water campsites.

The park is a lovely place to take kids for biking along a paved path, and short hikes; there are six marked trails they and less-abled folks can trundle along on that include interpretive signs describing the flora and fauna. The 1.6-kilometre Many Springs loop is a popular one in the summer, taking visitors up slight hills and past yellow ladyslipper orchids to a tiny, bubbling spring.

Flower buffs will enjoy the field around Middle Lake in late spring when it is dotted with bright red western wood lilies, but there are other fabulous flowers to look out for here too; just keep your field guide at hand. This loop is longer and not as flat, but you can still enjoy the view from a parking area above the lake if you don't feel like walking.

Another favourite easy tromp is the Flowing Water trail that follows the edge of the Kananaskis River from the Willow Rock campground. At the far end of the loop is a large beaver pond, but if you want to see one of the big-toothed rodents, walk in at sunrise or dusk. Muskrat, which are smaller than beavers and show their tails above water when swimming, also frequent the pond.

Details: *Go early for day trips, and definitely check www.tpr.alberta.ca/ parks/kananaskis/trailreport.aspx for trail conditions, including bear warnings. This IS the Rockies, after all. It's located 25 kilometres east of Canmore on Highway 1, then 0.5 kilometres north on Highway 1X.*

98 Crowsnest Pass

Right between Waterton Lakes and Banff National Park lies the Crowsnest Pass, an area brought into modern being because of coal and railways but which is kept alive because of the beauty of its location.

Avid snowmobile and ATV fans

flock to the pass for its 1,200 kilometres of mapped trails that run from the US border to Kananaskis Country following old logging and coal haul roads. For the downhill skiers, Castle Mountain is just 40 minutes away and there are plenty of cross-country ski trails, too.

During the snowless months, hikers and mountain bikers can take their pick of about 26 trails spread over 300 kilometres in the area, and there's fishing galore – just remember to check licensing rules.

History buffs will know the communities that line the crooked pass lived and literally died with coal, two in particular standing out in Albertan's memories.

A kilometre-wide swath of rubble marks the sombre site of the 1903 Frank Slide disaster where in less than two minutes one early April morning, 82 million tonnes of limestone crashed down from Turtle Mountain to bury part of the town of 600 people. Frank Slide Interpretive Centre commemorates the event with award-winning multi-media presentations.

Just up the road north of Frank is Hillcrest, site of Canada's worse mining disaster where 189 men lost their lives on June 19, 1914 when an explosion ripped through the Hillcrest mine. The disaster left 130 women widowed and 400 children fatherless in the small community of 1,000. The men were buried in three mass graves, which are marked. A monument was erected in 2000 to commemorate all the mining tragedies in Canada.

Details: *The Frank Slide Interpretive Centre is open year round and is fully wheelchair accessible. Call (403) 562-7388 for more information. It is located one hour west of Fort McLeod on Highway 3. Hillcrest is about 10 minutes north on Highway 3.*

Nikka Yuko Japanese Garden 99

Southwest Alberta is a hot, gusty place most of the year, subject to bone-dry summers and winds that can blow a 16-wheeler truck off the highway. So entering the serene greenness of the Nikka Yuko Japanese Garden in Lethbridge is like sake to a parched soul.

The four-acre oasis incorporates Japanese gardening philosophies and symbols with local flora and the southern Alberta landscape. The result is a harmonious balance where layered landscapes flow effortlessly around five traditional Japanese garden themes of trees, shrubs, rocks, waterfalls, ponds and bridges.

Nikka Yuko, which roughly translates as Japan-Canada friendship, commemorates the contributions of Japanese Canadians forcibly relocated and interned during World War II. It was designed in the mid-1960s by renowned Japanese landscape artist Dr. Tadashi Kubo who not only studied Lethbridge's prairie landscape with its wall of mountains to the west, but the people and culture of the area before creating the garden.

Each item in Nikka Yuko, from shrubs and boulders seemingly placed at random, to the teahouse and bridges built in Kyoto of aro-

TAKE 5 JIM MCLENNAN
A FLY FISHERMAN'S MUST LIST

Jim McLennan was one of the original fly-fishing guides on Alberta's Bow River, and one of the people who brought Trout Unlimited to Alberta in the 1970s. Since then, Jim and his wife Lynda (founding director of Casting for Life), have been teaching fly fishing, writing about fly fishing, photographing fly fishing and making presentations about fly fishing. McLennan has written four fly-fishing books and is a regular contributor to fly fishing magazines. More importantly, Jim's a guru of the rod who gently reminds us research and flies are good, but listening to what the river has to say is better.

1. One of the best things about Alberta is its glorious summer mornings. If you start your outdoor breathing before 8:00 am you'll know what I mean. Even in the most severe heat wave (yes, we get them), it doesn't matter how warm it is today, it will cool off overnight, and the sharp and unblemished morning air will provide a fresh start tomorrow.

2. The stoic and stately Porcupine Hills of the southwest are symbolic of the whole province's geography. Their west side is steep and treed, lying beneath the jagged Chinook-spillway known as the Livingstone Range. Their dry and treeless eastern side tilts more gently, its grassland marking the northwestern edge of the Canadian prairie.

3. Alberta has developed and attracted a group of uniquely gifted artists, especially musicians. Just a brief list includes Ian Tyson, Amos Garrett, Cowboy Celtic, Tommy Banks, and P.J. Perry. Unique, world-class artists who choose to make their homes and their music here.

4. For a fly fisher, the trout streams of Alberta are an undeniable attraction. The Bow, Crowsnest, Oldman, Ram . . . if I didn't live here, I'd move here just to be close to them.

5. The Alberta prairie in October is a combination of warm amber light, faint voices of geese and cranes, and the sweet aroma of cut grain. Autumn is like a benediction for the seasons and for the land, and is revered by those who seek reasons to spend it outdoors.

matic yellow cypress, was meticulously researched for its aesthetic and cultural value before being placed in exactly the right spot.

During the May to October season, visitors can take part in a tea ceremony, kite making, workshops by master Japanese gardeners and traditional Japanese festivals such as Tanzaku (when you can write a wish on paper and hang it on bamboo) or go moon-gazing during Tanabata, the star festival.

In tune with the garden's serenity theme, visitors are discouraged from using mobile phones or electronic games on site. Only water is allowed in the garden but beverages and snacks are available at the visitor's centre.

Details: *Located at 9th Ave South at Mayor Magrath Drive. For more information, call (403) 328-3511. Unfortunately, no wheelchairs, strollers, canes or shoes are allowed in the Pavilion due to the fragile flooring.*

100   Twin Butte General Store

There's a little bit of everything and a lot more than you expect at the Twin Butte General Store tucked in the south western-most corner of the province.

That the grocery store serves as the area's post office, liquor store and information centre shouldn't come as a surprise; these are the standard offices of a hamlet's mercantile in ranch country. It's the great Mexican food and make-you-wanna-get-up-and-dance live music that are beyond the usual and make this Canadian Twin Butte General Store a destination on its own.

Entertainers like Sam Baker, Mojave and the Justin Lacroix Band ply their musical trade in the store's restaurant, which serves up the meanest huevos rancheros this side of the border.

Owner, chef and all-around great guy Larry Davis also makes sure the breakfast sausage is chorizo, and the scrambled eggs are served on a flour tortilla spread with refried beans. Originally from southern California, Davis bought the then-abandoned store in the mid-1990s and built it up, literally and figuratively, to the store/restaurant/gift shop/music venue/bed and breakfast/campground it now is.

The Mexican fare of enchiladas, tacos, burritos and fajitas is so mouth watering, Twin Butte has become a must-stop on motorcycle trips and leisurely Sunday drives from urban centres such as Lethbridge and Calgary. Not into Mexican? Try the elk and buffalo burgers, a chicken wrap or some pizza before continuing on your trip to Logan's Pass and going to the Sun Road into Glacier Park, or the Remington Carriage Museum in Cardston.

The popularity of the general store is some accomplishment considering the resurrected 1932 store sits pretty much in the middle of nowhere between Pincher Creek and Waterton Lakes National Park. The road, though, is Highway 6, the tail end of the Cowboy Trail. Which means that this 'middle of nowhere' is flanked to the west by stunning mountain vistas and rolling hills spotted with wooded hollows to the east into the golden Prairies.

Details: *For more information, call (403) 627-4035, toll free at (866) 976-7378. Or go online at twinbuttestore.ca. From Lethbridge, take Highway 5 south for about 45 kilometers, then take Highway 6 north for another 27 kilometres. From Pincher Creek, take Highway 6 south for 27 kilometres.*

Priddis View and Brew   101

On a clear summer day there's little as glorious as the sight of rolling foothills, aspens fluttering in the breeze and a couple of guys on horses checking fences - unless you add a nosh from the Priddis View and Brew Bistro at the same time.

Located in a remodelled farmhouse just off the Cowboy Trail about 15 minutes southwest of Calgary, the café/bistro has a menu full of country staples with a twist, like mac 'n cheese with shrimp and scallop casserole (divine!) or the veggie sandwich on a multigrain bun. Friday's dinner is whatever the chef feels like cooking, most often comfort food of the best kind – full of calories and a loving hand with the seasoning.

The bistro's website jokes about dogs and horses being welcome as long as they're tied up, but owner Lynne Norem notes traffic on Priddis Valley Road West has become too busy to hitch animals up by the house safely. And she's not too keen about cleaning up the poop either, she often jokes.

Noren has lived in the valley for decades and offers a down-home welcome buffed shiny by a sophisticated palette and eye for art. She taps into local and regional artists to stock her small gift shop with unique gift items, or can point you to a nearby studio. In true country style, the View and Brew also has a video rental franchise, is the local vendor for bulk water, and is the courier depot for the Priddis community.

There only are five tables in the bistro and it's pretty popular with locals, so reservations are recommended for dinner. There still might be room at the counter, though, and a patio out back that is licensed for 60.

Details: *From Calgary take Highway 22X going due west, take a slight left (south) turn on Highway 22, then left again at Priddis Valley Road. Or check it out online at www.viewandbrew.ca.*

Create Your Own

1.

2.

3.

4.

5.

Ultimate Must List

6._____

_____

_____

_____

7._____

_____

_____

_____

8._____

_____

_____

_____

9._____

_____

_____

_____

10._____

_____

_____

_____

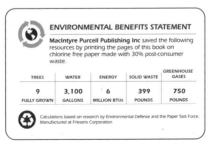